EMU:
THE LEGAL, I.T. AND
PRACTICAL ISSUES

AUSTRALIA
LBC Information Services
Sydney

CANADA and USA
Carswell
Toronto

NEW ZEALAND
Brooker's
Auckland

SINGAPORE and MALAYSIA
Thomson Information (S.E. Asia)
Singapore

EMU:
THE LEGAL, I.T. AND PRACTICAL ISSUES

General Editor
Richard Bethell-Jones

Sweet & Maxwell

Published in 1999 by
Sweet & Maxwell Limited of
100 Avenue Road
London NW3 3PF

(http://www.smlawpub.co.uk)

Typeset by Dataword Services Limited of Chilcompton
Printed in Great Britain by Bookcraft (Bath) Ltd

A C.I.P. catalogue record for this book
is available from the British Library

ISBN 0752 00671 1

No natural forests were destroyed to make this product,
only natural farmed timber was used and re-planted.

Foreword

This book has been written with a legal audience in mind. However, the law is not so complicated that the book would be inaccessible to people who are not lawyers. The book brings together all the various legal issues which arise in relation to the introduction of the single European currency. We have collected together in the Appendices much useful background material. We hope that this book will provide a single source of reference for those who have to deal with legal issues arising out of the introduction of the single currency.

Whilst the legal issues are important, the strategic, operational and I.T. issues which businesses will have to deal with are far more complex and difficult. Although the strategic and operational issues are beyond the scope of this book; we have included a chaper by Heather Rowe of Lovell White Durrant on certain of the practical and legal issues which arise in trying to sort out the I.T. requirements.

Geoffrey Yeowart of Lovells has provided the Chapter on the Equity Markets and Company Share Capital. Geoffrey has been involved on euro related issues right from the start; in particular as a member of the City of London Joint Working Group, which has provided significant input both to the U.K. Government and the European Commission on legal issues arising out of EMU.

Dina Albagli of Herbert Smith has provided the Chapter on Financial Instruments. It is in relation to Financial Instruments that EMU has the biggest legal impact. Our thanks to Dina for grappling with the intricacies of the ISDA Protocol, redenomination, renominalisation and harmonisation.

Emma Nendick, also of Herbert Smith, has provided the Chapter on tax. Although EMU is intended to be tax neutral, it is necessary to have an understanding of where tax consequences might arise.

The Introduction provides a brief overview of the history of monetary union, describes what will happen in the Transitional Period and analyses the legal framework for the euro. Chapter Two deals in general terms with continuity of contract — an issue which is of most significance in relation to financial instruments. The Introduction and Chapter Two are a kind of primer for the rest of the book.

It is beyond the scope of this book to consider any of the political and economic aspects of EMU. In particular it does not include an analysis of how the European Central Bank, in conjunction with the national Central banks of the participating Member States, will manage monetary policy or how particip-ating Member States will be held accountable for any fiscal deficits or government borrowing in excess of amounts allowed by the stability and growth pact.

There is a vast amount of written information about the euro and monetary union. One purpose of this book is to act as a sift of that material to concentrate on those things which have legal relevance. Set-out on the next page is a selective list of other material which readers may find useful. Much of this material was written when we did not know whether or not the U.K. would participate in EMU from the start. We now know that the U.K. will not join at the start. But the material is still relevant as a guide to what is happening in the countries which are joining and as a reminder of what will have to be done if the U.K. eventually joins.

On behalf of all the authors — we hope that you will find the book useful.

Richard Bethell-Jones
General Editor

Sources of Further Information

H.M. Government has produced a number of "euro factsheets" which contain a great deal of useful practical information on all aspects of EMU. Those factsheets can be obtained from website http://www.euro.gov.uk/facts.html.

For general background material, looking at the political and economic issues see:

- *The pros and cons of EMU* by David Currie — published by the Economist Intelligence Unit. An abridged version is available from H.M. Treasury.

- *A Cool Look at the Euro* by Samuel Brittan — published by the David Hume Institute.

For information on the effect of EMU on businesses generally see:

- *The Single European Currency — A practical guide* by The Hundred Group of Finance Directors.

- *EMU — Practical Information for Business* — H.M. Treasury, published in June 1997.

- *Preparing for the euro — A practical guide for professional and business managers* — published by the British Computer Society.

For information on the impact on accounting and information systems see:

- "Accounting for the introduction of the euro" — a European Commission paper produced by DGXV.

- "Preparing Information Systems for the euro" — a European Commission paper produced by DGXV although much of this information is covered by HMG's euro factsheets mentioned above.

For information relevant to financial markets:

- ISDA's EMU Guidebook is essential.

- "Economic and Monetary Union: Proposals for the equity markets" — The London Stock Exchange, January 1998.

- CREST and EMU — CREST Co. Limited, February 1998.

The Bank of England has published regular bulletins called "Practical Issues Arising from the Introduction of the Euro". These contain a wealth of very detailed and useful information about all issues relevant to the financial markets operating in the City of London. The Bank of England website (http://www.bankofengland.co.uk/piq.htm) contains a useful list of Internet addresses for information on the euro.

For an analysis of continuity of contract see the papers on that issue published by the Financial Law Panel. These include an analysis of the legal position under English law and certain jurisdictions outside the E.U.

The Business and Accounting Software Developers Association (BASDA) (website http://www.basda.org) has issued a number of useful I.T. related publications including a specification for application software and test data to help users ensure that their financial and accounting software can handle currency conversion in the way required by the euro regulations (that is using triangulation).

Contents

Chapter 1 — Introduction
by Richard Bethell-Jones, Wilde Sapte

Chapter 2 — Continuity of Contract
by Richard Bethell-Jones, Wilde Sapte

Chapter 3 — Tax Issues Arising from the Euro
by Emma Nendick, Herbert Smith

Table of Statutes

(All references are to paragraph numbers.)

Table of Statutory Instruments

(All references are to paragraph numbers.)

Table of European Legislation

(All references are to paragraph numbers.)

1

Introduction

by Richard Bethell-Jones, Wilde Sapte

Brief history of the single market and impetus for a single european currency

The programme for achieving monetary union between all or some of the Member States of the European Union was laid down in the Maastricht Treaty which was agreed in 1991. However, to find the real beginning of the impetus for monetary union, it is necessary to go back a further 21 years to 1970.

    In 1970, the Werner Plan proposed a ten-year programme to achieve a single currency. At that time, there were only six members of the European Economic Community — France, Germany, Italy, Belgium, Netherlands and Luxembourg. The Bretton-Woods Agreement, in place since immediately after the end of the Second World War, had maintained relatively fixed exchange rates between the West European currencies which made monetary union achievable.

    However, shortly after the Werner Report was issued, the Bretton-Woods agreement began to break down and, in 1973–74, the economies of Western European countries were severely disrupted when OPEC raised the price of oil. The economic instability which resulted from that increase in energy costs lead the governments of different countries to pursue different policies and, in some countries, those policies were highly inflationary. Lack of exchange rate stability made the achievement of monetary union quite impossible.

    In 1979 the European Monetary System (EMS) was introduced. Under that system, currencies could fluctuate in a range of plus or minus 2.25 per cent to a central ECU rate; although the currencies of some countries (Italy, Spain and the United Kingdom) were allowed to fluctuate within wider bands. By the end of 1986, the European Economic Community had been enlarged to 12 Member States. The members now included Denmark, Ireland, the United Kingdom, Greece, Portugal and Spain. The Single European Act of 1986 laid the foundations for the single market within the European Economic Community.

1.01

1.02

In 1989, the Delors Report proposed a plan for the achievement of monetary union within an Economic Community of 12 Member States. The Delors Report was the foundation for the provisions now contained in the Maastricht Treaty which, some 10 years after the Delors Report, will result in 11 of the now 15 Member States of the European Union participating in a single currency.

In the ten years to 1989, the EMS had worked reasonably well; which provided the basis for believing that the European Community could proceed to closer monetary union. But in 1992–93 various foreign exchange crises caused problems for the EMS. Sterling, having joined late in 1990, withdrew in 1992. Notwithstanding a certain amount of exchange rate turbulence in the early 1990s, the Member States of the European Community have continued the struggle to achieve the necessary economic convergence to allow the single currency to be introduced at the beginning of 1999.

The final stage on the road to monetary union has now started. At the beginning of May 1998, the heads of Government of the Member States of the European Union decided on which states would be the initial members of EMU. That decision was based on recommendations from the European Commission and ECOFIN; which had reviewed the performance of all Member States in relation to the convergence criteria laid down in the Maastricht Treaty. The decision was that 11 Member States would be the initial members. Those states are Austria, Belgium, Finland, France, Germany, Ireland, Italy, Luxembourg, Portugal, Spain and the Netherlands. This leaves out four E.U. Member States: the U.K., Denmark, Sweden and Greece.

1.03   Greece wants to join the single currency as soon as its economy allows, and is working hard to achieve the necessary economic convergence. The position of Sweden and Denmark is not clear; but it is likely that, if EMU is successful, both of those countries will want to participate in EMU.

The U.K., having negotiated a right to opt out of monetary union in the Maastricht Treaty, exercised its opt-out at the end of 1997 despite having met the convergence criteria better than a number of other Member States which will actually participate. The position of the current U.K. government is reasonably clear; and was set out in a statement made by the Chancellor of the Exchequer to the House of Commons on October 27, 1997.

In that statement, the Chancellor made it clear that there was no constitutional issue of principle which would stop the U.K. participating in EMU. The conclusion on the question of principle was "if, in the end, the single currency is successful, and the economic case is clear and unambiguous, then the Government believes Britain should be part of it". The Statement also set out five economic tests that will define whether a clear and unambiguous case can be made.

The Government has also stated that, because of the magnitude of the decision, there must be a referendum of the British people before the decision is finally taken. There will be no referendum before the next general election but, if the Government is minded to join, and feels that there is a reasonable chance of a referendum producing a vote in favour of joining, a referendum could be held fairly soon after the next election which must take place by May 2002 at the latest. It is possible, therefore, that a decision by the U.K. to join could be taken in 2002 or, just possibly, before the end of 2001.

Milestones on the road to monetary union

Progress to the Single Market

1.04

1951	Treaty of Paris. European Coal and Steel Community established.
1958	Treaty of Rome. European Economic Community established, including Belgium, France, Italy, Luxembourg, Netherlands, West Germany.
1970	Werner plan for European monetary union.
1972	"Snake" exchange-rate mechanism set up as Bretton-Woods system breaks down.
1973	Denmark, Ireland and U.K. join E.E.C.
1973/74	OPEC raise the price of oil — severe dislocation of European economies.
1979	European monetary system (EMS) founded, including exchange-rate mechanism (ERM).
1981	Greece joins E.E.C.
1986	Single European Act (SEA) lays foundation for single market. Portugal and Spain join Community.

From the Delors Report to Monetary Union

1989	Delors Report on Monetary Union.
1991	Maastricht Treaty agreed, leading to establishment of E.U. and setting out plans for EMU.
1992/93	Various exchange rate crises.
1994	European Monetary Institute established.
1995	Austria, Finland and Sweden join EU.
1997	Year for testing Convergence Criteria
1998	Start of Stage 3 European Central Bank comes into existence — replacing the EMI participating Member States chosen — based on convergence criteria
1999	Start of Transitional Period
2002	Euro finally replaces participating national currencies for all purposes

Timetable for the Final Phase and the Transitional Period

1.05   The so-called Stage 3 on the road to EMU started in May 1998 when the Convergence Criteria were tested and the Member States which would participate at the start were selected. It was agreed that the Transitional Period would start on January 1, 1999 and would last three years; with the final changeover happening at the beginning of 2002. Set out below is a summary of what will happen during Stage 3.

Phase A — January 1, 1998 to December 31, 1998

1.06   In May 1998, the Member States which will participate were announced; and it was also confirmed that the single currency will be introduced on January 1, 1999. Although the exchange rates between the currencies of the participating Member States were also announced, it will not be until December 31, 1998 that the fixed conversion rates between the participating currencies and the euro will be decided.

On May 3, 1998 the legal framework for the introduction of the euro was finalised; when the second of the two Council Regulations was issued; the first such Regulation having been issued in June 1997.

Phase B — January 1, 1999 to December 31, 2001

1.07   Phase B will take place during the three calendar years of 1999, 2000 and 2001 known as the Transitional Period.

At the start of the Transitional Period:

(a) Exchange rates of participating currencies and the euro are locked.

(b) The euro becomes the currency of the participating Member States.

(c) The European Central Bank assumes responsibility for monetary policy.

(d) All new government debt is denominated in euro.

(e) Wholesale payments are made in euro.

During the three-year period:

(a) National notes and coins still circulate as legal tender — but as sub-divisions of the euro.

(b) Banks and financial institutions continue to change to the euro.

(c) Public and private operators proceed to switch to the euro as and when they wish.

There is a policy of no compulsion/no prohibition for the private sector during the Transitional Period. Full and free conversion between the euro and participating national currencies at the fixed exchange rates is obviously an essential requirement during this phase and must be provided not only by the central banks but by the banking system generally.

During the Transitional Period it will only be possible to pay in cash using national notes and coins. However, where payment is to be made by credit transfer, the payer can (in certain circumstances) choose to pay either in the national currency unit or in the euro unit.

Phase C — First Half of 2002

The final phase — lasting only six months — is due to start on January 1, 2002. **1.08** During that six months' period euro notes and coins will be put into circulation and national notes and coins will be withdrawn. It is only during this six months' period that cash payment can be tendered either in national currency notes and coins or in euro notes and coins.

At the end of the Transitional Period all monetary amounts denominated in a participating National Currency unit will be converted to euro units at the official conversion rate.

Legal framework for the euro — the two regulations

In order to set out the legal status of the euro and provide a framework for the **1.09** introduction of the euro, two Council Regulations have been instituted.

The first is Council Regulation (E.C.) No. 1103/97 of June 17, 1997. This Regulation was made under the powers in Article 235 of the Treaty on European Union. It is sometimes called the Article 235 Regulation; but it is also known, and will be referred to in this book, as the "First Regulation".

The second is Council Regulation (E.C.) No. 974/98 of May 3, 1998. It was made under Article 109.l(4) of the Treaty on European Union. It is sometimes known as the Article 109.l(4) Regulation but it is also known, and will be referred to in this book, as the "Second Regulation".

Why are there two Regulations? Originally there was to be only one Regulation promulgated under Article 109 of the Treaty on European Union. However, it was then discovered that, because of the way the U.K. and Danish opt-outs worked and the fact that other Member States would not join, a Regulation made under the powers in that Article would only apply in those Member States which actually participate in the single currency. It was therefore necessary to split off those matters which needed to apply in all Member States, even if they were not joining, and provide for those in a separate Regulation made under Article 235 of the Treaty.

The First Regulation

The First Regulation applies in all Member States whether they participate in **1.10** the single currency or not. It deals with three things. First, the replacement of the "official" ECU by the euro; second, continuity of contract; and third, it sets out a method for converting between the participating national currencies and the euro and for rounding.

The full text of the First Regulation can be found in Appendix 1 to this book. It contains definitions of "legal instruments", "participating member states", "conversion rates", "national currency units" and "euro units".

Replacement of the ECU by the euro

1.11   Article 2 of the First Regulation provides for the replacement of the ECU by the euro at a rate of one euro to one ECU. This is discussed in more detail in Chapters 2 and 4. It is important to note that it is only what is known as the "official" ECU which is replaced in this way. Any contracts which define amounts by reference to a "private" ECU will continue in accordance with their terms.

Continuity of contracts

1.12   Article 3 contains the all important provision which "reinforces legal certainty and clarity" and "confirms the principle of continuity of contracts and other legal instruments". Again this article is dealt with more fully in Chapter 2.

Conversion and rounding

1.13   Articles 4 and 5 deal with conversion and rounding. Conversion rates are to be adopted as one euro expressed in terms of each of the national currencies of the participating Member States. Those rates are adopted with six significant figures. The final Conversion Rates will only be known on December 31, 1998.

Note that the requirement is that Conversion Rates be adopted with six significant figures — not to the nearest six decimal places. Thus, typical conversion calculations could be as follows:

> 1 euro = FF 6.58001
> 1 euro = DM 1.92003

These are not the exact Conversion Rates (which will only be finally known on December 31, 1998).

Conversion Rates must not be rounded or truncated when making conversions, and the Conversion Rates are to be used for conversions either way between the euro unit and the national currency units.

Inverse rates derived from the Conversion Rates are not to be used; because, apparently, using inverse rates can give rise to distortions. Also, monetary amounts to be converted from one national currency unit into another must first be converted into an amount expressed in the euro unit (which can be rounded to not less than three decimal places) which is then converted to the other national currency unit. This is known as "triangulation". No alternative method of calculation is allowed unless it produces the same results.

1.14   It can be seen that the First Regulation provides a very precise method of converting. There are also specific provisions relating to rounding in Article 5 of the First Regulation. Where an amount has been converted into the euro unit odd amounts are rounded up or down to the nearest cent. Monetary amounts converted into a national currency unit are rounded up or down to the nearest sub-unit (or in the absence of a sub-unit to the nearest unit, or according to national law or practice to a multiple or fraction of the sub-unit or unit) of a national currency unit. In either case, where the application of the Conversion Rate gives a result which is exactly half way, the resulting sum must be rounded up.

It is obviously useful to have a closely defined set of rules for conversion and rounding which are applied throughout all Member States of the European

Union. Software which is designed to carry out conversion between national currency units and the euro must comply with the requirements of these rules or, at least, produce the same result.

It is not clear why inverse rates are not allowed or why, when converting from one national currency unit to another, there must be two stages; first, converting to the euro unit and then to the second national currency unit. There may be some mathematical explanation as to why, unless you follow those prescribed methods, inaccuracies may occur.

As is mentioned in Chapter 6, existing computer systems which deal with foreign currencies, and which are able simply to include the euro as an additional foreign currency are quite likely to use inverse rates when converting and are unlikely to have the ability to go through the two stage process when converting from one national currency unit to another. However, so long as the same results are produced, it cannot matter what method is used to produce the result.

The Second Regulation

The full text of the Second Regulation can be found in Appendix 2 to this book. It is divided into six Parts. What each Part deals with is briefly described below: **1.15**

- Part I contains definitions used in the Regulation. The "Transitional Period" is defined as the period from January 1, 1999 to December 31, 2001.

- Part II deals with: **1.16**

  (a) The substitution of the euro for the currencies of the participating Member States.
  (b) Adopting the Conversion Rate between each participating currency and the euro.
  (c) Adopting the euro as the unit of account for the European Central Bank and of the central banks of participating Member States.

- Part III deals with: **1.17**

  (a) The status of national currency units during the Transitional Period.
  (b) How payments are made during the Transitional Period.
  (c) Redenomination of government debt and private debt.
  (d) Confirmation that netting and set-off will apply between euro units and national currency units; with any conversion being effected at the Conversion Rates.

- Part IV deals with: **1.18**

  (a) The introduction of euro bank notes and coins.

(b) The final substitution of references to the euro unit for all references to national currency units (according to the relevant Conversion Rates). This happens at the end of the Transitional Period on December 31, 2001.

(c) Withdrawal of bank notes and coins denominated in national currency units.

Status of the euro and national currency units

1.19   It is important to note that as from January 1, 1999 the currency of all participating Member States will be the euro. The currency unit is one euro; and one euro is divided into 100 cent.

At the start of the Transitional Period there will be no euro bank notes or coins; those will not be introduced until the beginning of 2002. So, during the Transitional Period all cash payments will have to be made in bank notes or coins in the old national currency units. Also, there will be a huge number of contracts which will contain obligations expressed in national currency units; and, indeed, during the Transitional Period (particularly at the beginning), new contracts will be entered into which express monetary amounts in the old national currency units.

However, although national currency units will still be used, this does not mean that there is a dual currency in the participating Member States. The only currency will be the euro; but it will be expressed in two forms. It can be expressed in euro and cent (decimalised sub-divisions of the euro) or it can be expressed in national currency units which are non-decimalised sub-divisions of the euro.

The Principle of No Compulsion/No Prohibition

1.20   During the Transitional Period parties are to be free to express monetary obligations in the euro unit; but they are not compelled to do so and are quite free to express their obligations in national currency units.

Article 6(2) provides:

"Where in a legal instrument reference is made to a national currency unit, this reference shall be as valid as if reference were made to the euro unit according to the Conversion Rates."

Article 7 provides:

"The substitution of the euro for the currency of each participating member state shall not in itself have the effect of altering the denomination of legal instruments in existence on the date of substitution."

Article 8(1) provides:

1.21   "Acts to be performed under legal instruments stipulating the use of or denominated in a national currency unit shall be performed in that national currency unit. Acts to be performed under legal instruments stipulating the use of or denominated in the euro unit shall be performed in that unit."

The provisions of Article 8(1) are subject to anything which the parties may have agreed.

In summary, during the Transitional Period, although the euro has become the currency of the participating Member States, during the early part of the Transitional Period, that will be barely noticeable to private individuals who will continue to use cash, and may continue to express their monetary obligations, in the form of national currency units.

Equally, anyone who wishes to transact business in the euro will be free to do so; and it is likely that the financial markets and big business will move to transacting business in the euro early on in the Transitional Period.

Using the euro for Credit Transfers
As we have seen, monetary amounts can still be expressed in national currency units, and if they are so expressed, the obligation will be to pay in the national currency unit (unless something else has been agreed). However, this is subject to an overriding provision in Article 8(3) of the Second Regulation. This is a very significant provision which is likely to lead to a great increase in using the euro unit for the purpose of making payments by way of credit transfer.

1.22

Article 8(3) provides a flexible method for making payments by credit transfer. It applies where:

    (i)   an amount is denominated either in the euro unit or in the national currency unit of a particular participating Member State; and

   (ii)   that amount is payable within that particular Member State by crediting an account of the creditor.

In this situation the debtor can pay either in the euro unit or in the national currency unit. Thus, if the debtor has to pay DM to an account in Germany it can choose whether to pay in DM or in the appropriate number of euro units using the Conversion Rates. Similarly, if the obligation is to pay in euro, the debtor can choose to pay in the appropriate number of DM. This does not work if the debtor has to pay DM in France (or any participating Member State other than Germany). It only operates where the payment has to be made in euro or in the national currency unit of the Member State in which the payment is to be made.

So far as the recipient/creditor is concerned it makes no difference what unit the payer pays in; because the amount must be credited to the recipient/creditor's account in the denomination of that account. In other words, if the creditor has a DM account but the payment is made in euro; the credit will turn up in the creditor's account in DM.

This Regulation obviously compels the bank receiving the payment to make the conversion; but it does not compel the bank receiving the payment to make that conversion free of charge. There has been a great deal of discussion between the various banking federations within Europe about charging for conversion and the general feeling is that, for most purposes, banks will not make a charge for conversion in relation to accounts of their own customers.

The Final Provisions

1.23   At the end of the Transitional Period, which ends on December 31, 2001, two things happen.

First, by Article 14 of the Second Regulation, all references to national currency units are replaced by references to the euro unit according to the relevant Conversion Rates and using the rounding rules. It is only at this stage that all monetary amounts in national currency units are redenominated in the euro unit.

Secondly, bank notes and coins denominated in national currency units will be withdrawn during the first six months of 2002. Individual Member States may shorten that six months period by their own national law if they wish. In addition, Member States are expected to enact their own rules and regulations in relation to accepting back bank notes and coins in exchange for euro after the end of that six months (or any shorter) period.

Redenomination of Government Debt

1.24   The Second Regulation authorises participating Member States to take measures to redenominate their government debt in the euro unit and to facilitate other debt issuers to redenominate the debt which they have issued. This obviously requires individual national legislation in each participating Member State.

2

Continuity of Contract

by Richard Bethell-Jones, Wilde Sapte

Introduction

This Chapter looks generally at the question of continuity of contract. Not unnaturally, continuity of contract has given rise to most concern in relation to financial contracts which are dealt with in detail in Chapter 4. There is inevitably some overlap between the two Chapters — but this Chapter can perhaps be regarded as a primer for those who want to get involved with the detail in Chapter 4 which assumes a reasonably sophisticated knowledge of the issues.

2.01

At an early stage in thinking about preparations for the single currency, lawyers identified continuity of contract as perhaps the single most important legal issue. What would happen to a contract which provided for payment to be made in, for example, French Francs; if the French Franc no longer existed? What about a contract swapping an interest payments on a notional amount of French Francs with interest payments on a notional amount of Deutschmarks (exposing the parties to both interest rate and currency movements); or to a forward foreign exchange contract between two currencies replaced by the euro.

Dealing with changes to the currency of a country was not a new problem. At various times, countries have changed their currencies; and most states have evolved legal principles to deal with that. Those principles recognise that the law of the state whose currency has been changed will determine what happens to payment obligations. Again, to take an example, if an obligation to pay 100 old French Francs is replaced with an obligation to pay 10 new French Francs according to the laws of France — then other countries will give effect to that change when enforcing an obligation to pay French Francs which is contained in a contract governed by their own domestic law. That countries should have adopted this approach is not very surprising. It recognises that the law governing payment of monetary obligations should be governed by the law of the state whose monetary obligations are involved. This is the so called *lex monetae* principle.

2.02

Originally, the European Commission was not proposing to do anything special in relation to the issue of continuity of contract when the single currency replaced the currencies of participating Member States. The Commission regarded the matter as something which would fall into place by the operation of existing legal principles. However, the Commission were eventually persuaded that the matter was of such vital importance that steps ought to be taken to clarify what happens when financial obligations are affected by the introduction of the euro. As a result, the First Regulation was introduced which, among other things, dealt specifically with continuity of contract. The relevant provision is Article 3 of the First Regulation.

The First Regulation

2.03   The First Regulation came into effect on June 17, 1997. Note that this is a Regulation — not a Directive. We are generally more familiar with Directives such as the Banking Co-ordination Directive, the Investment Services Directive, the Data Protection Directive and many others. The significance of a Regulation is that it has direct effect in all Member States of the E.U. as soon as it comes into effect; whereas a Directive requires Member States to implement their own national law or regulation to give effect to the terms of the Directive — a process which takes a long time and often produces slight (or more than slight) differences in the various Member States.

The First Regulation deals with three things which are relevant in all Member States whether or not they participate in the single currency. First — the replacement of the ECU by the euro. Second — continuity of contract. Third — rules for conversion of national currency units to the euro and vice versa; and dealing with how odd amounts are to be rounded.

The First Regulation is reproduced in full in Appendix 1 to this book. Before going on to discuss that continuity regulation it is worth highlighting one of the Recitals in the preamble to the regulation. This is Recital 7 which states as follows:

"Whereas it is a generally accepted principle of law that the continuity of contracts and other legal instruments is not affected by the introduction of a new currency; whereas the principle of freedom of contract has to be respected; whereas the principle of continuity should be compatible with anything which parties might have agreed with reference to the introduction of the euro; whereas, in order to reinforce legal certainty and clarity, it is appropriate explicitly to confirm that the principle of continuity of contract and other legal instruments shall apply between the former national currencies and the euro and between the ECU . . . and the euro; whereas this implies, in particular, that in the case of fixed interest rate instruments the introduction of the euro does not alter the nominal interest rate payable by the debtor: . . ."

2.04   This Recital does two important things. First it makes it clear that the regulation is not thought to change the law of any Member State. The

regulation simply confirms the principle of continuity of contract and reinforces legal certainty and clarity. Secondly, and helpfully, the Recital makes it
clear that, in the case of fixed interest rate instruments, the introduction of the
euro will not alter the nominal interest rate payable by the debtor.

There had been particular concern about long-term fixed interest rate
contracts denominated in currencies prone to inflation. If the currency of the
contract is prone to inflation (for example, Italian Lira) the nominal interest rate
for such a contracts tends to be high; simply to reflect the devaluation of the
amount lent. The euro is expected to be a relatively hard currency; and both
long and short term interest rates for euro denominated loans are expected to
be relatively low and stable. A question arose as to what would happen when
the original (inflationary) currency was replaced by the euro. Debtors would be
unhappy having to continue to pay high fixed rates of interest and might seek
to terminate or change the terms of those loan contracts on some basis. The
Recital makes it clear that such an argument is not expected to succeed.

Article 3 — Continuity of contract

Article 3 of the First regulation state as follows: **2.05**

> "The introduction of the euro shall not have the effect of altering any term
> of a legal instrument or of discharging or excusing performance under any
> legal instrument, nor give a party the right unilaterally to alter or terminate
> such an instrument. This provision is subject to anything which parties may
> have agreed."

It can be seen that the Article is very straightforward. It provides that the
introduction of the euro will not have the effect of altering a legal instrument
— or of discharging or excusing performance under any legal instrument. Nor
will it give a party the right unilaterally to alter or terminate a legal instrument.

The Regulation provides that "legal instruments" shall mean legislative and
statutory provisions, acts of administration, judicial decisions, contracts, unilateral legal acts, payment instruments other than bank notes and coins, and
other instruments with legal effect. This is a very comprehensive definition,
and explicitly includes all contractual commitments of all kinds.

Clearly, if the parties to a contract have chosen to provide that the
introduction of the euro will have the effect of altering its terms or discharging
or excusing performance, or give a party the right to alter or terminate that
contract; such a provision must be capable of being enforced on the basis that
the principle of freedom of contract must be respected. For this reason, the final
sentence of Article 3 provides that that Article is subject to anything which the
parties may have agreed.

With this simple and basic background, are there likely to be any problems
in relation to particular contracts or types of contract; or in relation to
particular types of provision which may be found in some contracts?

Why might there be any problems with continuity? — English Law Principles

In considering this issue in relation to contracts governed by English law, it is   **2.06**
necessary to have in mind the English law principles which might cause or

allow a court to hold that a contract should be terminated or changed when there is nothing specifically in the contract allowing that to happen. As is the case in most jurisdictions, English law will, in most cases, enforce a contract strictly in accordance with its terms even if circumstances change. The courts will not re-write the contract just because one party finds the contract is working harshly. However, in some cases this produces such obvious injustice that the courts have established two basic principles to mitigate that strict rule. One is based on implied terms and the other is the doctrine of frustration.

Implied Terms

2.07   An example of a term being implied into a contract to give business efficacy to that contract (which is particularly relevant to EMU) arose when the Bank of England stopped publishing Minimum Lending Rate ("MLR") in 1991. At that time they were very many contracts in existence under which interest was payable at a rate which was fixed by reference to MLR. Were all those contracts to become inoperative because there was no mechanism for the calculation of the rate of interest under the contract? Although the matter never came before the courts, the prevailing view was that the courts would accept an argument to the effect that a reference to MLR would be treated as a reference to clearing bank base rate. As a matter of commercial reality; clearing bank base rate was, in effect, what MLR had been.

In other words, in order to give business efficacy to the contract, the courts would allow the substitution of a commercially reasonable alternative to the price-fixing mechanism which had disappeared. This view was so obviously correct that it never became necessary to test it before the courts.

Frustration

2.08   The doctrine of frustration allows a party to a contract to escape from its obligations if it has become impossible to perform those obligations or it no longer makes commercial sense to do so. However, it is clear that the courts are very reluctant to agree that a contract has been frustrated. A frustrating event must be an extraneous event or a change of situation which takes place without fault on the part of the person seeking to rely on it. In addition, it must be something which they did not or could not have contemplated when they entered into the contract. In the context of EMU, the general feeling is that most reasonably sophisticated people would have been aware that EMU was likely to happen at or shortly before the Maastricht Treaty, so that no party to a contract entered into after about 1991 could reasonably claim that the advent of EMU (or its consequences) was a frustrating event. Clearly there could, certainly in theory, be exceptional circumstances where a particular consequence of EMU could not have been foreseen even later than 1991 and the particular consequence is so unfair that the courts should give relief; but despite thinking hard, no-one has come up with an obvious situation where that is likely.

Possible problems with continuity

The first thing to be said is that no real problems with continuity have been **2.09**
identified. The purpose of this Chapter is, perhaps, to rehearse those arguments which have been put forward as a basis for asserting that a contract will
or may not continue unaffected by EMU, and then to show how such
arguments will not (or are unlikely to) succeed.

These issues are dealt with under the following general heading:

(a) Events associated with EMU.

(b) Force majeure, change of circumstances and similar clauses.

(c) ECU-denominated contracts.

(d) Non-E.U. law contracts.

Events associated with EMU

To paraphrase, Article 3 of the First Regulation provides that "the introduction **2.10**
of the euro" shall not effect, etc., a contract. Those with minds to split hairs
(and where a very large sum of money is at stake such minds exist) saw that
this provision did not explicitly cover events other than the introduction of the
euro but which would inevitably flow as a consequence.

For example, fixing the conversion rate between participating currencies (like
the Deutschmark and the French Franc) would be a consequence of the
introduction of the euro; but it could be argued that it was not specifically
covered by Article 3. Similarly, the introduction of the euro will eventually lead
to the disappearance of the interest rates known as FIBOR and PIBOR (which
will be replaced by a new rate known as EURIBOR). That is a consequence of
the introduction of the euro but is something different from the actual
introduction and not specifically mentioned in Article 3.

What then would happen to such things as forward foreign exchange
contracts designed to hedge currency movements when currencies no longer
moved; or to contracts providing for the calculation of interest by reference to a
price source that had disappeared. For most contracts this issue will not be
relevant. However, for large financial contracts and in particular for swaps and
derivative contracts, the possibility of these matters being argued about is
unpleasant.

It is likely that the result under English law, even without the assistance of **2.11**
Article 3 of the First Regulation, would be that this kind of contract would
have continued. It would not have been frustrated. A contract to swap
amounts or streams of income in different currencies which both disappeared
and were replaced by the euro would turn into an annuity stream. Where a
price source disappeared the courts, if the parties could not agree, would imply
a term to replace the disappeared price source with a reasonable commercial
substitute.

However, to meet any doubts about these matters, and to give additional
contractual certainty, the International Swaps and Derivatives Association
published their own continuity provision. That provision is reproduced in

Appendix 2 to this book. It can be seen that this contractual provision expands considerably on the terms of Article 3. In framing this provision ISDA had in mind that somebody might enter into a contract believing that EMU would take place and then find that it did not. The clause therefore deals "the occurrence or non-occurrence of an event associated with Economic and Monetary Union".

2.12   ISDA have also produced a "Protocol" under which parties to swap and derivative contracts can agree what will happen when price sources disappear. The continuity provision and the protocol are discussed in more detail in Chapter 4.

These initiatives by ISDA are designed to give as much contractual certainty as is possible in relation to high value complex financial instruments; and are important for the markets in which those instruments are traded. However, it is worth mentioning that, as with the First Regulation itself, it is arguable that this is unnecessary; and that all that these provisions do is set out what a court would say the position would be if called upon to do so. These provisions do not alter anyone's legal position; just make it impossible (or very difficult) for someone to argue the toss. In eliminating unmeritorious claims and argument these initiatives are valuable; but parties to a contract which does not incorporate these sophisticated provisions need not think that they are at great risk or that their position is necessarily different.

Force Majeure, Change of Circumstance and Similar Clauses

2.13   As already noted, Article 3 of the First Regulation provides that the continuity provision is subject to anything which the parties may have agreed. The question therefore arises as to whether standard force majeure, change of circumstance or market disruption clauses might enable a party to get out of a contract. They would argue that the existence of this kind of clause showed that the parties had agreed that the contract would not continue unaffected by EMU.

In considering this question it is useful just to think about what contracts people might want to get out of. An obvious example would be a long-term fixed interest rate contract at a rate which was higher than prevailing market rates. Another example is a party to a derivative contract seriously out of the money and with little or no prospect of the situation changing. A party to such a contract would search diligently through it to try and find some provision which might enable him to prepay without penalty or claim that the purpose of the contract had been frustrated and that the contract should be ended. Will he succeed? The truth is that no-one can be absolutely certain. It will depend on the wording of the clause and on the circumstances in which the party to the contract is trying to invoke that clause. However, despite giving the question a considerable amount of thought, no-one has come up with a contract or a situation where that is likely to happen. The general consensus is that, for most contracts, typical force majeure or change of circumstance clauses will not allow termination or renegotiation of the contract.

Obviously, if a clause in the contract specifically provides that the introduction of the single currency (or some other event associated with or consequential upon that happening) will allow termination or a change to that contract then that clause will be given effect to. However, again, it has not been possible to find examples of contracts where such a clause has been included or where it would be appropriate in any circumstances which can be reasonably contemplated.

ECU–Denominated Contracts — a real problem

Article 2 of the First Regulation provides that every reference in a legal instrument to the ECU (as referred to in Article 109(g) of the Treaty and as defined in Regulation (E.C. No. 3320/94) will be replaced by a reference to the euro at the rate of one euro to one ECU. It then goes on to provide that references in a legal instrument to the ECU will be presumed to be references to the "official" ECU — but that such presumption will be rebuttable. It follows that, where the contract defines the ECU as what is known as the "private" ECU (being the ECU at a defined moment in time rather than as it changes from time to time) the reference to the "private" ECU will not translate to the euro on a one to one basis.

2.14

It is important to be aware that it may well make a significant economic difference as to whether an obligation to pay or quantify an amount by reference to the ECU does translate from one ECU to one euro (which it will do if the references to the "official" ECU); or whether the obligation will continue to be calculated by using a basket value comprising a number of currencies (some of which will have been replaced by the euro). Although one euro will have the same value as one ECU on January 1, 1999. The values will soon be different. This is because the currencies which make up the ECU are not the same as the currencies which will form the single currency. It will therefore be critical as to whether a reference in a legal instrument is to the official ECU or to a private ECU; because the economic consequences will be different if a payment has to be made or an amount quantified sometime after January 1, 1999. It is inevitable that there will be some disputes on this issue.

It has to be said that this is unfortunate. There has been a real interference with the economic substance of the bargain between the parties to the contract. All would have been well (or certainly better) if the currencies which merge into the euro were the same as those which made up the ECU and no others. The conceptual approach of the Commission in deciding that the euro would replace the ECU on a one to one basis proceeded on the assumption that that would happen; but, as things have turned out, that is not the case.

2.15

Possible additional problems in relation to ECU denominated obligations arise because the ECU is not a currency as such; it is merely a measure of value. This means that the *lex monetae* principle will not be applicable, and this increases uncertainty about how an obligation would be treated under a contract governed by the law of a non-E.U. Member State. Although it has been said that the approach within the E.U. and the provision about one to one conversion in the First Regulation may be "persuasive" and cause the courts of non-E.U. jurisdictions to adopt the same approach; the truth is that other jurisdictions may not take kindly to a relatively arbitrary interference with the real economic substance of a contract.

Non-E.U. Law Contracts

2.16   The First Regulation only applies in Member States of the E.U. Where a contract is governed by some other law, the question of continuity of that contract will fall to be decided under the principles of that other law. As already mentioned, the principal of *lex monetae* (or its equivalent) is widely recognised in most jurisdictions, so continuity ought not to be a problem in other jurisdictions.

The Financial Law Panel has carried out research into the position under the law of a limited number of jurisdictions which are significant for financial contracts to see if the law of those jurisdictions would produce a result which was different to that contemplated by the First Regulation.

Whilst no-one can be certain of what the legal position would be in relation to all kinds of contract and all types of contract wording; the general picture is reassuring. The positions have been researched in some detail in Japan and Switzerland. Both those jurisdictions produce results which are surprisingly similar to what the results would have been under English law had the First Regulation not existed. And, as we have seen, the First Regulation is not thought to have made any change to English law.

In the USA the States of New York, Illinois and California have introduced their own continuity legislation. It is not dissimilar to the E.U. First Regulation and certainly has the same intended effect of giving assurance about continuity whilst preserving the freedom of contract to provide otherwise. It is surprising that some U.S. States have gone to the trouble of introducing domestic legislation to deal with a change of currency in some states in Europe. Nowhere else was this thought to be necessary or appropriate.

Summary

2.17   Rightly so, the issue of continuity of contract has given rise to much concern. It is terribly important; particularly in the financial markets. However, without wishing to be unduly complacent, the truth is that it should not present a problem. Domestic law of most jurisdictions would not allow a contract to be set aside just because, for example, Germany of France replace the DM or the FF by the euro. The First Regulation reinforces legal certainty and lays a number of possible doubts to rest. Those involved with swaps and derivatives can make use of the ISDA initiatives to minimise, if not altogether eliminate, unmeritorious and costly disputes.

Continuity Clauses

2.18   If you have a contract which includes provisions for payments to be made in, or monetary amounts to be determined by reference to, a currency which is going to be replaced by the euro, is it necessary to include a clause that makes it clear that the contract will continue after the change of currency unaffected save for the substitution of the new currency for the old at the relevant conversion rate?

For most contracts governed by the law of a E.U. member State the answer is clearly no! Given that (a) continuity was never a problem anyway (because of the *lex monetae* principle) and (b) the Commission has, nevertheless, been kind enough to issue a regulation (the First Regulation) which confirms the principle of continuity of contract and reinforces legal certainty and clarity; it would be utterly perverse to then find it necessary to add a clause into a contract of the kind described to provide for continuity yet a third time. However, pressure to be seen to be euro aware often means that a clause to confirm continuity is inserted.

If such an unnecessary clause is to be inserted, it is important to make sure it does not do any damage. The danger is that because the continuity Article provides for continuity of contract "subject to anything the parties may have agreed" there is a possibility that an unfortunately worded continuity clause might let in the argument that the intention was to agree something different to what Article 3 provides, producing uncertainty instead of certainty. For most contracts therefore the best advice is don't include a continuity clause. If such a clause is to be included, keep it simple and track the wording of Article 3 closely. An example clause would be:

> "The parties confirm that the introduction of the euro shall not (i) have the effect of altering any term of, or discharging or excusing performance under, this Agreement or (ii) give a party the right unilaterally to alter or terminate this Agreement."

Where the contract is governed by the law of a jurisdiction other than an   **2.19**
E.U. Member State there may be more reason to include a continuity clause. Again, it should not be necessary; the principle of *lex monetae* doing what is necessary. But remember that *lex monetae* may not work where the obligation is expressed in ECU. For those few jurisdictions which have passed their own continuity legislation it will be best, if a clause is to be included at all, to follow the wording of the relevant legislation.

Note the cautious use of "most" — a continuity clause is not necessary for "most" contracts. When might such a clause, or a clause more elaborate than a simple repetition of Article 3, be a good idea? Well, derivatives are an obvious example and ISDA has produced its own response in the form of the ISDA continuity clause and the Protocol (see Appendix 2). Other examples do not spring to mind. There may well be contracts of a type which might, on ordinary principles of frustration, not survive EMU despite the principle of *lex monetae* and the First Regulation. But, if English law principles based on frustration allow the contract to terminate or change, that is because fairness demands that; so inserting a continuity clause would have been inappropriate and the parties would not have agreed to the clause going in.

3

Tax Issues Arising from the Euro

By Emma Nendick, Herbert Smith

Introduction

EMU will have immediate tax implications for any U.K. business which has any involvement with currencies which will convert to the euro. This is so even though the U.K. will not be "in" on January 1, 1999. In particular, those trading with countries whose currencies convert to euro, or borrowing from or lending into such countries or dealing in currencies which convert to the euro will all be affected.

3.01

U.K. tax law and practice in relation to the euro and EMU are still evolving and no doubt will continue to do so as understanding of the issues increases. The Inland Revenue ("I.R.") has had extensive discussions with a number of taxpayer bodies in the accounting, financial and other sectors with a view to identifying issues, formulating policy and, where necessary, changing the law.

In general the approach of the I.R. "is to try to ensure as far as possible that the introduction of the single currency in other Member States is tax neutral and therefore does not give rise to a charge or a loss which would not otherwise have arisen" (I.R. Press Release, July 29, 1998). To this end, a number of legislative changes have been announced and draft Regulations are expected to be published in the Autumn. A number of useful indications of I.R. practice have also been given.

U.K. tax issues raised by the euro covered in this Chapter fall into six main areas:

3.02

(a) tax treatment of euro conversion costs;

(b) tax compliance, including VAT;

(c) re-denomination of debt and equity denominated in a converting currency;

(d) re-denomination of sterling denominated debt and equity into euro;

(e) implications of conversion for other existing contracts and assets.

(f) international tax planning.

A seventh section deals with some miscellaneous issues.

This chapter makes extensive reference to I.R. Press Releases of January 21, July 29 and July 31, 1998. These Press Releases are reproduced in Appendix 3.

Tax Treatment of Euro Conversion Costs

3.03   U.K. businesses having any dealings with the euro will necessarily incur costs in adapting their internal systems. These changes may range from ensuring that their word processing package includes the euro symbol to adaptation of their computer systems to allow payments to be made and receipts recorded in euro, or, for financial institutions, to allow dealing, borrowing and lending in euro. The majority of these costs are likely to be in the area of computer software adaptation. Other costs may include adapting machinery, such as slot machines and cash tills, to accept payments in euro, and staff and customer training.

From a tax perspective there are two issues here:

(a) will businesses be entitled to tax relief for these costs?

(b) will businesses be entitled to credit for input VAT incurred on these costs?

Tax relief for conversion costs

3.04   A trader will be entitled to an immediate deduction for conversion costs, provided two conditions are satisfied:

(a) the sums are incurred on revenue, rather than capital, account; and

(b) the sums are paid wholly and exclusively for the purposes of the trade.

A trader which incurs conversion costs which are capital, rather than revenue, will be entitled to capital allowances for that expenditure provided:

(i) it is expenditure on the provision of machinery or plant wholly and exclusively for the purposes of the trade; and

(ii) as a consequence of incurring the expenditure the machinery or plant belongs to the trader (Section 24 of the Capital Allowances Act ("CAA") 1990).

Capital expenditure incurred by a trader on acquiring a right to use computer software or on acquiring software outright for the purposes of the trade is treated as expenditure on plant and machinery which belongs to the trader (Section 67A of the CAA 1990). Plant and machinery allowances are generally given on a 25 per cent per annum reducing balance basis. If one assumes expenditure of 100 in year one, the trader is entitled to immediate relief of 25 in year one, 18 in year two (18 being 25 per cent of 75) and so on.

Investment companies, as defined in Section 130 of the Income and Corporation Taxes Act ("T.A.") 1988, will be entitled to a deduction in the period in which payment is made for conversion costs which constitute management expenses (Section 75 of the T.A. 1988). Investment companies are also entitled to capital allowances in respect of capital expenditure on machinery or plant used for the purposes of management of the business (Section 28 of the CAA 1990). By virtue of Section 28, Section 67A of the CAA applies to expenditure by investment companies on computer software, with the necessary adaptations for investment companies.

The accounting treatment adopted for conversion costs, although not necessarily determinative of the tax treatment, will be influential in determining whether expenditure is treated as revenue or capital for tax purposes. In particular, it will in practice be more difficult to obtain a revenue deduction for expenditure if the expenditure has been capitalised in the accounts. Indications from the ASB's Urgent Issues Task Force (Abstract 21) are that conversion costs should be expensed immediately through the profit and loss account unless the company already has a policy of capitalising expenditure of that type or that expenditure clearly results in an enhancement of the relevant asset beyond merely maintaining its service potential.

The IR has stated that it intends to set out in Regulations exactly what will be allowable as a deduction, at least in relation to the costs of redenomination of investments (see I.R. Press Release, July 29, 1998). The following is based on the law as it currently stands.

Software conversion costs

Expenditure on software developed in-house is treated in the same way for tax purposes as software developed by an independent software house. The same principles also apply whether the software is licensed to users or acquired outright.

3.05

The I.R. has stated (in *Tax Bulletin*, Issue 34; see also the I.R. Inspector's Manual) that purely conversion driven costs required in adapting systems to the euro are unlikely to be capital in nature. These costs should therefore be immediately deductible from trading profits as a revenue item. They will include the costs of modifying information technology systems which deal with management and financial accounting and with payments and regulatory processes. Banks will incur additional costs relating to changes to settlement and clearing systems. Interfaces with the BACS, SWIFT and CHAPS systems will also be affected. TARGET, the cross-border euro settlement system (linking CHAPS and its equivalent systems), is to be introduced for use throughout the EEA. Banks' existing clearing systems will require adapting to interface with the new system. All the above costs, if purely conversion driven, will be revenue deductible items.

However, where conversion driven costs are overtaken by the development of new business systems for strategic reasons, for example, to exploit changes in the financial markets accompanying the introduction of the euro in order to open up new trading opportunities, the project may be capital in nature, rather than revenue (I.R. Tax Bulletin, Issue 34). Having established that a project is capital in nature will not necessarily mean that all expenditure associated with it will be treated as capital, although the bulk of the cost is likely to be so.

3.06   In this situation capital allowances should be available on a 25 per cent per annum reducing balance basis for part of the expenditure and a revenue deduction may be available for other parts of the expenditure. As a basic guide, the following (based on the I.R. Inspector's Manual, March 1997) is likely to be the treatment of the various stages of system development of a capital software development project:

(1) Initial research expenditure and preliminary planning. Although such expenditure may be capital, in many cases it will not be possible to show that expenditure at this stage is incurred on the capital asset. As such the expenditure is unlikely to qualify for capital allowances.

(2) Practical test and trial exercises.

(3) Design and development of full working systems.

Stages (2) and (3) are likely to be capital in nature and eligible for capital allowances, provided Section 67A of the CAA is satisfied.

(4) Costs associated with implementation (especially staff training).

(5) Upgrading, updating and error correction.

Expenditure on stages (4) and (5) is likely to be revenue and therefore immediately deductible.

Other costs

3.07   (a) **Staff training and customer information:**

The costs of training staff to use new or upgraded software, and to understand the implications of the euro for the business, are likely to be revenue deductible items. Likewise the costs of informing customers about changes being introduced in relation to the euro should be revenue deductible.

(b) **Costs of adapting machinery:**

By analogy with the position regarding updating of software, a revenue deduction should be available for the cost of adapting, for example, slot machines and cash tills to accept the euro, provided the adaptation is purely conversion driven.

(c) **Interest on a loan to fund conversion costs:**

This will generally be deductible for companies. Deductions will be allowed under the loan relationships rules on either an accruals basis, if the company adopts an accruals basis of accounting, or on a due and payable basis, where the company uses a mark to market basis of accounting (Sections 82–85 of the Finance Act ("F.A.") 1996).

VAT Input Tax Recovery

Where a business incurs conversion costs, it is likely to be charged VAT in relation to some of them. For example, an external software house will charge VAT in relation to software adaptation work.   **3.08**

The question then arises as to whether the business is entitled to recover or to receive credit for the input VAT suffered. The starting point is that credit is only given for input VAT which is used exclusively in making standard rated or zero rated supplies (Section 26 of the Value Added Tax Act 1994). In most cases it is unlikely that VAT incurred on conversion costs will be directly attributable to specific supplies. It is likely, however, that a proportion of the VAT incurred will be recoverable as a general overhead. The proportion will generally be determined according to the overall ratio which the value of taxable supplies made by the business bears to all supplies made by the business in the relevant accounting period (Regulation 101(2)(d) of the VAT Regulations 1995), unless the business has agreed a different partial exemption method with H.M. Customs & Excise. Where a business makes only taxable supplies, this should lead to full recovery of input VAT on conversion costs. Note that full input tax recovery is unlikely to be possible in relation to the redenomination of debt and equity. (See paragraphs 3.20 and 3.24 below.)

Tax Compliance

Paying tax in euro

Legislation has been passed which enables the Treasury to make regulations allowing payments of tax to be made in euro (Section 163(3)(a) of the F.A. 1998). Businesses will be able to pay tax, VAT and National Insurance contributions tax in euro from January 1, 1999 (I.R. Press Release, July 31, 1998). The currency risk will be borne by the taxpayer: the relevant revenue department will convert the payment received into sterling at the prevailing rate and credit the taxpayer with the sterling value. Bank charges for converting euro payments into sterling will be borne by the revenue departments. Payment can be made by cheque, BACS or CHAPS. Consultation on the detail of the arrangements is continuing: this includes consideration of how to collect underpayments or repay overpayments which arise as a result of currency fluctuations.   **3.09**

Submitting tax returns in euro

At present the Government has no plans to allow the general body of taxpayers to submit tax returns computed in euro. However, companies which have made a functional currency election ("FCE") under section 93 of the F.A.   **3.10**

1993 and the Local Currency Elections Regulations 1994[1] can compute their tax liability in the foreign currency in respect of which they have made an FCE. These provisions will be extended to allow companies to make an FCE in relation to the euro for accounting periods beginning on or after January 1, 1999 provided the conditions in the Local Currency Regulations are satisfied (see I.R. Press Releases of January 21, 1998 and July 29, 1998 and Section 163(3)(b) of the F.A. 1998). Regulations 5 and 6 of the Local Currency Regulations set out the conditions which must be satisfied before a company can make an FCE. In particular, only trading companies can make an FCE and they can only do so if the relevant currency is the currency of the primary economic environment in which the trade is carried on and, broadly, the accounting or financial statements of the trade are drawn up in that currency. Regulations will be made to ensure that FCEs in relation to currencies which convert to the euro will automatically carry over to the euro for the company's first accounting period ending after January 1, 1999 in which the company prepares its accounts in euro (I.R. Press Release, January 21, 1998 and Section 163(3)(c) of the F.A. 1998).

The I.R. has said that the ability to make an FCE will not be extended to non-trading companies (I.R. Press Release of July 29, 1998).

Invoicing in euro — VAT

3.11   U.K. businesses may find themselves under commercial pressure to price and invoice in euro. This raises VAT issues because, although businesses will be able to account for VAT in euro from January 1, 1999, they will not be able to operate entirely in euro for VAT purposes.

This is because a VAT invoice must state in sterling the amount of VAT chargeable (Regulations 14(1) and (2), VAT Regulations 1995, S.I. 1995 No. 2518). Even if dual invoicing in both sterling and euro is adopted, it is the sterling VAT figure which fixes the trader's output VAT liability and which must be included in the VAT return. Where customers pay in euro, the trade is therefore exposed to a currency fluctuation risk to the extent sterling moves against the euro after the VAT invoice has been issued. Given that the VAT liability must be computed in sterling *vis-à-vis* H.M. Customs & Excise, accounting for the VAT to H.M. Customs & Excise in euro will not eliminate the currency risk. Businesses may attempt to reduce the risk by encouraging customers to pay early or by hedging. Consultation is still continuing on detailed arrangements for payments of tax in euro so it is possible that the position may change.

The way in which rounding differences (when converting sums between sterling and the euro) are dealt with in the dual invoicing process will also have an impact on the euro amount of VAT charged and therefore on the exchange risk.

---

[1] The Local Currency Elections Regulations 1994 (S.I. 1994 No. 3230).

Redenomination of Debt and Equity Denominated in a Converting Currency

Redenomination of debt: continuity for holders

The I.R. has said that straightforward redenomination into euro of bonds **3.12** denominated in currencies which join EMU will not normally give rise to a tax charge that would not otherwise arise (I.R. Press Release January 21, 1998). Further details included in the I.R. Press Release of July 29, 1998 indicate, however, that the issue is not cut and dried. The I.R. stated that to the extent that the investor in taxed under the rules for taxing foreign exchange gains and losses (FOREX rules), the financial instrument rules or the loan relationships rules in relation to the debt, the IR would expect the accounts to be followed, subject to any express statutory rules (I.R. Press Release of July 29, 1998).

For corporate investors the position is therefore as set out below.

Accounting rules should not require any further recognition of FOREX profit or loss between annual translations.

The European Commission has issued guidance on accounting for the euro ("Accounting for the introduction of the euro", June 1997). The introduction of the euro will not, in the Commission's view, alter the relationship between the currency units of a participating member state and the currency of a non-participating country such as the U.K. In these cases the currencies continue to fluctuate against one another and the exchange differences on these balances are treated in the same manner as was previously the case.

Therefore, where previously a company had been recognising fluctuations in value between, for example, sterling and a French Franc denominated bond, from January 1, 1999 the company will recognise fluctuations in value between sterling and the euro equivalent of the French Franc principal amount as at January 1, 1999. The ASB's Urgent Issues Task Force Abstract 21 confirms that, as SSAP20 requires continues recognition of gains and losses on all monetary assets, there is no reason to recognise any additional accounting profit or loss on conversion.

The accounting rules can be overridden by specific tax rules, but it would seem that the U.K.'s rules on taxing foreign exchange gains and losses in F.A. 1994 ("the FOREX rules") should not trigger an additional tax charge.

The FOREX rules require a company to bring in for tax purposes FOREX gains and losses on qualifying assets whenever an accrual period ends in relation to an asset (Section 125 of the F.A. 1993). An accrual period ends whenever an accounting period ends or whenever a company "ceases to be entitled to an asset" (Section 158 of the F.A. 1993).

The question therefore is whether conversion leads to a company ceasing to be entitled to the asset. It is arguable that it does not. The company still holds an investment in the French company with the same principal amount. It is simply denominated in a different currency. In fact the question is academic because, even if the company does cease to be entitled to the French Franc bond, it immediately becomes entitled to a new asset, that is the bond denominated in euro. As the FOREX rules require annual recognition of FOREX profits and losses, this should mean that conversion triggers no additional tax charge or loss.

3.13   *Example:* Company X has a March 31 year end. On April 1, 1998 it held a bond with a principal amount of 1000 French Francs. The sterling value of the bond at that point was £700. At midnight on December 31, 1998 the sterling value of that bond has fallen to £650. On March 31, 1999 the sterling value of the bond has gone up to £800.

Ignoring conversion one would normally take the value in sterling of the bond at the beginning of the accounting period and its value at the end of the accounting period and bring in the difference. In the example this would lead to a FOREX profit of £100. If conversion triggers an extra translation time (because the company is treated as ceasing to be entitled to the bond) does this trigger a further tax charge or loss? It should not. At December 31, 1998 the company records a sterling loss of £50 but then immediately becomes entitled to an asset worth £650. At March 31, 1998 it records a sterling profit of £150. This leads to an overall sterling profit of £100 for the year ended March 31, 1999, *i.e.* the same result as occurs if conversion does not trigger an extra translation time.

The FOREX element of the bond is taxed under the FOREX rules and for corporate holders the remainder will generally be taxed under the loan relationship rules. Will the loan relationships rules require the company to bring in a profit or a loss as a result of conversion? As with the FOREX rules, the loan relationships rules will look first to the accounting treatment of conversion. A company is required to bring in for tax purposes all profits, gains and losses arising from its loan relationships as determined in accordance with an authorised accounting method (Section 84 of the F.A. 1996). This will be the accruals basis for most companies. There is no published accounting guidance on the non-FOREX accounting implications of conversion. However, it seems unlikely that, for accounting purposes, an investor would be required to recognise a disposal of the "old bond" and the acquisition of a replacement — the bond is still the same investment with the same principal amount. However, the redenomination is a disposal or an acquisition of rights or liabilities under the loan relationship the application of statute could lead to a tax charge or loss even where the accounts do not require a profit or loss to be recognised. This is because, in these circumstances, the redenomination would be a "related transaction" under Section 84(5) of the F.A. 1996, the profit or loss from which must be brought in in the accounting period in which the related transaction occurs.

The question of whether redenomination gives rise to a disposal will depend upon principles of contract law determining whether a change to the terms of a bond are merely a variation or are so fundamental as to lead to rescission of the old contract and creation of a new contract. If the existing terms of the bond envisage redenomination it is unlikely that redenomination will lead to a disposal. The question is less straightforward where the original terms of the bond do not envisage redenomination, although the E.U. regulation on continuity of contract may assist to avoid a disposal. This is discussed in more detail in Chapter 2 — "Continuity of Contract". In addition, although in law there may be some doubt as to whether a disposal is triggered, it appears from the I.R. Press Release of July 29, 1998 that the I.R. may consider that there should not be a loan relationship charge. This can be deduced from the need (perceived by the I.R.) to legislate to avoid a charge where the bond is taxed under the capital gains tax rules, rather than the loan relationships rules. The implication of this is that if the I.R. considered that a loan relationships charge could arise, legislation would be introduced to avoid it.

Where the holder is taxed under the capital gains tax rules in relation to the debt, the I.R. considers that redenomination could give rise to a taxable gain or loss but accepts that it is not desirable for a tax charge to arise on a straightforward redenomination consequent on the introduction of the single currency (I.R. Press Release, of July 29, 1998). The I.R. therefore proposes to introduce a regulation to ensure that if an asset is redenominated into euro and the post-redenomination asset is in all material respects the same as the pre-redenomination asset, then redenomination will not be regarded as involving a disposal or acquisition and the asset will be regarded as the same asset for chargeable gains purposes, *i.e.* a form of reorganisation treatment will be available. If other changes are also made to the debt (beyond those required for a straightforward redenomination), then, on general principles this may give rise to a disposal (see above).

Even if reorganisation treatment is available, redenomination could still trigger a tax charge where the "old" bond is a qualifying corporate bond ("QCB") acquired on a hold-over under Section 116 of the Taxation of Chargeable Gains Act ("TCGA") 1992, as redenomination would lead to the held-over gain coming into charge (Section 116(9)). Also, Section 116(8A) of the TCGA provides that there will be a tax charge under the loan relationships rules in F.A. 1996 on the basis of a disposal of the "old" bond at its market value. It is possible that these issues may also be addressed in legislation.

Redenomination of debt: rounding payments

It is unlikely that a round number of French Francs, in the example, will convert into a round number of euro. This means that the issuer may choose to make cash rounding payments made to investors.   **3.14**

Where the investor is taxed under the loan relationships rules in relation to the bond, it should not be taxed on rounding payments provided that they constitute a partial repayment of the debt.

Where the investor is taxed under the capital gains tax rules in relation to the bond, the payment will be treated as a part disposal. However, the I.R. proposes to introduce a *de minimis* exception for cash payments received on a redenomination as a result of the introduction of the single currency. There is no indication yet as to what level this excemption may be set at.

Redenomination of equities denominated in participating currencies

This issue will be relevant for companies holding shares in companies located in the euro zone. The I.R. has not published detailed guidance in this area and   **3.15** will not do so until it becomes clearer how redenomination will be achieved. The clear implication from the July 29, 1998 Press Release, however, is that redenomination of non-sterling denominated shares into euro would be treated as a reorganisation for tax purposes and therefore should not trigger a disposal. It remains to be seen whether an exemption will be introduced for cash rounding payments. By analogy with the position in relation to debt, an additional FOREX charge should not arise on redenomination of equities.

Redenomination of Sterling Denominated Debt and Equity

3.16   Redenomination of the share capital of U.K. companies into euro is not likely to be a widespread issue unless and until the U.K. is "in". By contrast, companies wishing to take advantage of the euro debt market may wish to redenominate sterling debt into euro sooner than this.

The tax implications of the redenomination will depend upon how redenomination is achieved. The principal questions are:

(i)   whether redenomination will constitute a disposal by the holder of the original bond or share, thus potentially triggering a tax charge;

(ii) if a disposal is triggered, whether any gain arising on the disposal can be deferred (possibly through the availability of reorganisation treatment), at least until disposal of the redenominated bond or share; and

(iii) the tax treatment of the costs of redenomination and of any rounding payments.

Redenomination of debt: continuity for holders

3.17   The I.R. has said that straightforward redenomination into euro of bonds denominated in currencies which join EMU will not normally give rise to a tax charge that would not otherwise arise.

There appears to be no logical reason why this tax neutral treatment should not be extended to sterling debt which is redenominated into euro, at least once sterling is committed to convert. Therefore one would expect the treatment of sterling debt to be similar to that of non-sterling debt (with the exception of FOREX considerations). Therefore where the holder is taxed under the loan relationships rules in relation to the debt, the I.R. would expect the accounts to be followed subject to any express statutory rules. Given the I.R. concern to avoid a capital gains charge on a redenomination, it is hoped that a loan relationships charge could also be avoided.

Where the holder is taxed under the capital gains tax rules in relation to the debt, redenomination could give rise to a tax gain or loss but, as noted earlier, the I.R. accepts that it is not desirable for a tax charge to arise on a straighforward redenomination consequent on the introduction of the single currency and will legislate to avoid it (I.R. Press Release July 29, 1998). It is hoped that this will be extended to redenomination of sterling debt, at least during a sterling transition period.

The tax treatment of the incidental costs of redenomination and of rounding payments is dealt with in paragraphs 3.20 to 3.23 below.

Redenomination of sterling shares: continuity for shareholders

As stated above, it seems unlikely that U.K. companies will wish to redenominate sterling share capital into euro until a decision has been taken on the U.K.'s membership of the single currency.   **3.18**

The DTI, in a consultative document published in January 1998, discussed a number of ways in which redenomination of shares could be achieved. The tax implications will depend upon the route chosen. The alternatives under current law include:

(a) Cancellation of existing shares and issue of euro-denominated shares. This could be unattractive to shareholders under current law as it would constitute a disposal of the original shares, possibly triggering a tax charge, although the Government may in this event legislate to provide relief. Also, the cancellation procedure is lengthy and cumbersome under U.K. company law, requiring in particular, an application to court.

(b) The buyback of existing shares and issue of euro-denominated shares. For a shareholder the tax treatment could be the same as for a cancellation and fresh issue, *i.e.* unattractive. Also, the company will incur a stamp duty or stamp duty reserve tax cost of 0.5 per cent of the purchase price. Again, this route raises a number of company law difficulties.

The DTI has announced that it proposes to introduce a new simplified share redenomination procedure. This would allow a company to resolve that references in any document to share capital denominated in one currency will be to the equivalent amount in euro. A shareholder resolution will normally be necessary, although a board resolution will suffice if the company is redenominating into euro during any Transitional Period to sterling membership of the single currency. Companies would not be obliged to issue new share certificates after redenomination.

The I.R. appear to envisage that a redenomination would be treated as a reorganisation (see I.R. Press Release, July 29, 1998, note to questions at paragraphs 9.22 and 9.23). See paragraphs 3.24 and 3.25 below for the tax treatment of incidental costs of redenomination and of rounding payments.

Costs of redenomination of debt and shares

These will fall into two main categories: **3.19**

(a) The incidental costs of carrying out the redenomination. These may include lawyers and other advisers' fees, statutory fees (*e.g.* Companies House), costs of informing creditors and shareholders and costs of printing and sending out new share/bond certificates. The issue here is whether the issuing company will be entitled to tax relief for these costs.

(b) Rounding payments. Units of sterling debt/share capital are unlikely to convert into whole numbers of euro and it is possible that issuers will make rounding payments to creditors/shareholders in order to issue a round number of euro debt or shares. The issues here are (i) whether the issuer will get tax relief for these payments and (ii) whether investors will be taxed on them.

Incidental costs of redenominating debt

3.20   The following is based on current law.

The deductibility of these costs will generally depend upon the loan relationships rules in Section 84 of the F.A. 1996. Strictly, for relief to be available, it will be necessary for the costs to be incurred under or for the purposes of a loan relationship or a related transaction which includes a disposal of the loan relationship. Technically, there may be some doubt as to the availability of relief if the original bond did not envisage the redenomination and the redenomination does not amount to a disposal of the existing bond. However, the I.R. have stated (in *Tax Bulletin,* Issue 25) that costs directly incurred in varying the terms of a loan relationship are deductible. This is consistent with the statement in the I.R. Press Release of July 29, 1998 (question at para. 9.32) that the I.R. will regard the costs of redenomination as falling within Section 84(3) of the F.A. 1996.

The issuer will be entitled to credit for input VAT suffered in relation to the redenomination of debt only to the extent the redenomination debt is issued to non-E.U. persons (The VAT (Input Tax) (Specified Supplies) Order 1992, S.I. 1992 No. 3123).

Debt and rounding payments

3.21   (a) **Tax treatment of the issuer:**

There may be some doubt as to whether rounding payments are incurred "directly" in varying the loan relationship in the same way that are, say, advisers' fees. It could be argued that rounding payments are a consequence of the variation rather than incurred directly in making the variation. However, such payments should be deductible on the basis of the I.R. Press Release of July 29, 1998 (see para. 3.20 above).

(b) **Tax treatment of investors:**

For investors receiving rounding payments, the position will be broadly as follows:

3.22   (i) U.K. individuals: Under existing law, a cash rounding payment could trigger a capital gains tax liability for individuals. However, the I.R. proposes to introduce a *de minimis* exemption for cash payments received on redenomination (I.R. Press Release of July 29, 1998, question at para. 9.23).

3.23   (ii) U.K. corporates: It seems that U.K. corporates should not be taxed on rounding payments under the loan relationships rules provided they constitute a partial repayment of the bond. However, if the old bond is a non-QCB and falls within the capital gains tax rules the de minimis exemption referred to above is likely to remove any tax charge.

Incidental costs of redenominating share capital

Under current law the company is unlikely to obtain a deduction for the incidental costs of redenominating its share capital into euro. However, the I.R. has indicated that it will be introducing a special relief for the cost of redenominating non-sterling equities. It is therefore possible that this relief will be extended to the costs of redenominating sterling equities into euro, particularly during a sterling Transitional Period. The issuer will be entitled to input VAT credit for VAT suffered in relation to the redenomination only to the extent that redenominated shares are held by non-E.U. persons.

3.24

Shares and rounding payments

(a) **Tax treatment of the issuer:**

3.25

The issuing company is unlikely to be entitled to a deduction for rounding payments.

(b) **Tax treatment of shareholders:**

Shareholders are likely to be taxed upfront on rounding payments either as a distribution or as a repayment of share capital.

Tax Implications of Conversion for Other Existing Contracts and Assets

Clearly the tax implications of conversion to the euro will depend upon the precise terms of the relevant contract and these will need to be examined in each case. A number of common transactions are considered below.

3.26

Borrowings

Assume a U.K. company has borrowed French Francs and this loan will continue after December 31, 1998. On conversion, the Franc becomes a denomination of the euro and the exchange rate between the Franc and the euro will be fixed. Conversion should have no significant tax implications for a U.K. borrower. Under the FOREX rules, the borrower will have been taxed and relieved on FOREX profits and losses on the loan annually (according to whether sterling has appreciated or depreciated against the Franc). From January 1, 1999 the borrower will be taxed and relieved on its FOREX profits and losses annually according to how sterling appreciates or depreciates against the euro. It seems unlikely that the conversion itself will trigger any additional tax charge or loss. The I.R. has also confirmed that the conversion should not trigger the FOREX anti-avoidance rules in Sections 135–136 of the F.A. 1993 (loss disregarded if main benefit of the transaction, non-arm's length transactions). See I.R. Press Release of January 21, 1998.

3.27

Trading obligations

3.28   A U.K. company buys goods or services under a continuing contract and pays for them in a currency which converts into euro. After conversion the obligation to pay that currency becomes an obligation to pay euro (albeit that payments can still be made in the old currency during the Transitional Period). This conversion should have no particular direct tax implications for the U.K. buyer. It will merely report any FOREX profits or losses as sterling appreciates or depreciates against the euro, rather than against the old currency.

Derivatives

3.29   Conversion will have particular tax implications for derivatives involving two currencies which both convert to euro on January 1, 1999. In many cases conversion will fundamentally alter the nature of these types of contract and this will flow through to the tax treatment.

         For example, a fixed Deutschmark/French Franc swap continuing over conversion will, unless the terms of the swap state otherwise, become, after that date, a stream of payments payable by the party which is out of the money on the conversion date. Each party will be able to calculate its final (or ultimate) FOREX profit or loss on the swap at that point as thereafter there can be no further fluctuations in value between the Deutschmark and the French Franc.

         From a tax perspective the question is: when will that FOREX profit or loss be taxed or relieved?

3.30   In most cases the answer will depend on how normal accountancy practice treats the profit or loss (Sections 126 and 159 of the F.A. 1993). The ASB's Urgent Issues Task Force Abstract 21 and guidance published by the European Commission ("Accounting for the introduction of the euro", June 1997) indicate that the accountancy treatment of the profit or loss will depend upon the purpose for which the swap is held. If it is purely speculative, it is likely that the whole of the FOREX profit or loss should be recognised and therefore taxed in the accounting period of the company in which conversion falls. However, if the purpose of the swap is to hedge a future liability it would be acceptable accounting practice for the FOREX profit or loss to be deferred until the accounting period in which the hedged liability is recognised. The tax charge or loss should therefore only crystallise at this point.

         The financial instruments legislation provides that "qualifying payments" which include swap payments, can be made without withholding of tax by a qualifying company — section 174 of the F.A. 1994. The I.R. has stated that fixed rate swaps of two currencies which convert to the euro will continue to be qualifying payments within the financial instruments legislation provided that no abuse is taking place (I.R. Press Release of January 21, 1998). The effect of this is that the payments can continue to be made gross, rather than becoming subject to withholding as an annuity or annual payments for tax purposes.

         The January 21, 1998 and July 29, 1998 I.R. Press Releases deal with a number of other detailed issues relating to derivatives, including options, currency contracts, interest rate contracts and futures and options which are subject to Schedule 5AA of the T.A. 1988 (guaranteed returns).

International Tax Planning Issues

Double Taxation Relief — Overseas FOREX Differences

On January 1, 1999 all exchange differences between converting currencies will **3.31** be frozen. The E.C. paper on accounting for the euro states that these exchange differences will generally be realised for accounting purposes. In jurisdictions which tax exchange differences on a realised basis, this may accelerate a tax charge or a tax deduction. Groups with exposure in these countries will therefore need to monitor the position in these countries.

The realisation of exchange differences has a number of knock-on U.K. tax effects:

- Where exchange differences are treated as realised, this will lead to an adjustment of distributable profits in the overseas subsidiary. Where this results in an increase, companies which are obliged to distribute a proportion of their profits may have to borrow in order to do so and may also face a tax bill. Conversely, where this results in a loss a dividend block may occur.

- The double tax credit attached to dividends from euro zone subsidiaries may also be affected. The tax credit is calculated by reference to the foreign tax borne on the "relevant profits" which the relevant overseas subsidiary has made. Relevant profits for these purposes are, broadly, commercial profits which a company can legally distribute (Inland Revenue Company Taxation Manual para. 8411). Relevant profits will therefore be affected by the amount of tax which a company suffers. As a result, where a tax charge or loss in the overseas jurisdictions is realised on conversion, this may cause the tax credit to go up or down.

    If the tax credit exceeds the U.K. corporation tax rate, companies could consider mixing dividends from these companies with dividends carrying a credit lower than the U.K. corporation tax rate in a mixer company, in order to avoid wasting overseas tax credits.

Transfer pricing

The U.K. transfer pricing rules broadly allow the I.R. to substitute an arm's **3.32** length price for tax purposes in intra-group transactions. Many other countries also have similar rules. The introduction of the euro may lead to intra-group supplies of goods and services (including intra-group borrowing) being priced in euro. This will clearly lead to greater price transparency and companies will need to be in a position to justify price differentials from country to country for transfer pricing purposes. Clearly pricing in euro is not going to eliminate basic production cost differences but groups do need to beware where transfer pricing policies have in the past been largely justified on the basis of exchange differences.

A particular transfer pricing issue is the pricing of European treasury activities. A significant part of the activity of a European treasury company may, in the past, have been currency hedging. Once the euro is introduced the need for this will be greatly reduced. This means that transfer prices charged by treasury centres to group companies will need to be reviewed and, if necessary, adjusted if they are to withstand scrutiny.

Cash pooling

3.33   The introduction of the euro is likely to make cash pooling more common across European groups. There are two main types of cash pooling.

The first is notional cash pooling. All the group companies have accounts and relationships with their local bank. Interest is charged and credited to them in their balances in the normal way. The bank then calculates its overall position *vis-à-vis* the group and charges interests as if all balances were pooled in one account. On the basis that this leads to a lower overall interest rate, an adjusting payment is made to a specified account or accounts, normally held by the treasury company.

The treasury company must then divide this payment up between the various group companies.

The tax issues that arise here are:

- Tax treatment of the payment by the bank to the nominated account. If this is characterised as commission the treasury company will be taxed on it (subject to double tax treaty relief) but it should not generally be subject to withholding.

- For transfer pricing purposes, the treasury company needs to ensure that the rebate from the bank is allocated between the group companies on an arm's length basis.

- Tax treatment of the payment by the treasury company to group members. In some jurisdictions, this may be characterised as interest. This may in turn give rise to a withholding liability (subject to double tax treaty relief).

The other type of cash pooling is cash concentration. Each group company still has a bank account but at the end of each day all monies on each account are swept into the group treasury's account. The bank then charges or credits interest only on this concentrated account. This method establishes intra-group balances which change each day. These will need to be operated on an arm's length basis for transfer pricing purposes which means that interest should be paid where appropriate and this may be subject to withholding. Thin capitalisation rules may also be relevant if cash pooling results in companies having excessive borrowings from other group members.

Other Issues

Matching Elections

3.34   A company may choose to hedge a foreign currency asset with a foreign currency liability or currency contract. Under Schedule 15 of the F.A. 1993 and the Exchange Gains and Losses (Alternative Method of Calculation of Gain or Loss) Regulations 1994[2] exchange movements on an eligible liability or currency contract may, in these circumstances, be deferred until, for example, disposal of the matched asset. The I.R. has confirmed that redenomination of the matched asset should not cause matching elections to become ineffective and so should not crystallise any deferred exchange movements (I.R. Press Release of January 21, 1998).

Repos and stock lending

Where a debt security denominated in a participating currency is redenominated, the redenominated security will, in all straightforward cases, be regarded either as similar or equivalent to the original security for repo/stock lending purposes.

3.35

---

[2] The Exchange Gains and Losses (Alternative Method of Calculation of Gain or Loss) Regulations 1994 (S.I. 1994 No. 3227).

4

Impact of the Euro on the U.K. Equities Markets and Company Share Capital[1]

by Geoffrey Yeowart, Lovell White Durrant

The introduction of the single European currency on January 1, 1999 in 11 E.U. Member States, will have far reaching implications for companies whose shares are traded in London, even though the U.K. has decided not to join in the first wave of membership. The London Stock Exchange and CREST have announced new facilities to respond to the needs of companies and investors. Changes to English company law are also being considered by the Department of Trade and Industry (DTI) to assist those companies that decide to redenominate their share capital to the euro.

4.01

Expected market trends

The introduction of the euro will result in major changes to the European capital markets, although it is not easy to evaluate the precise impact on the U.K. while it remains outside the euro area. Research carried out by the London Stock Exchange[2] suggests that large investment institutions — whose liabilities are predominantly in sterling — are likely to adopt a cautious attitude, pending a firm decision on U.K. entry. This approach is driven in many cases by the requirement to match assets and liabilities in the same currency. Retail investors are also expected to continue to trade shares in

4.02

---

[1] This chapter is based on an article contributed by the author to the *Journal of International Banking Law*, August 1998, published by Sweet & Maxwell. It has been revised and updated in the light of subsequent developments.

[2] "Economic and monetary union: proposals for the equity markets" issued by The London Stock Exchange, January 1998.

sterling until full U.K. entry. In contrast, continental investors may well diversify their shareholdings more widely on a euro area basis. They will be able to invest in a wider pool of equities in their domestic currency. This may lead to equities in the euro area being increasingly classified by sector rather than country. Pan-European indices are also expected to attract increasing attention.

It is expected that:

(a) Although most U.K. securities will continue to be traded in sterling while the U.K. remains out, some U.K. companies may want to change the currency of their share price to euro or even redenominate their share capital to euro before the U.K. joins.

(b) Continental investors in U.K. securities may wish to be able to trade and settle in euros.

(c) If the U.K. decides to join the euro area, a rapid switch to the euro is expected in the wholesale markets.

The Treaty on European Union does not expressly provide for separate transition periods for member states which join in a second or subsequent wave. However, it seems reasonable to assume that, if the U.K. were to join subsequently, it would be given a separate transition period on a similar basis, although its duration might be significantly less than three years. If the U.K. has its own transition period, the redenomination of share capital from sterling to euros is not expected to be mandatory until the end of the U.K. transition period.

London Stock Exchange and CREST

4.03   The currency in which shares are denominated and the currency of the prices in which they are quoted and traded on the London Stock Exchange need not necessarily be the same. It is perfectly possible for a share to be denominated in sterling and traded at a price in a different currency if the Stock Exchange provides this facility.

The London Stock Exchange, in its consultation paper of January 1998, invited comments from market participants on different options. One option was to offer dual trading in the 106 largest U.K. companies that are listed on the FTSE Eurotop 300 index. Investors would have the choice of buying or selling the relevant shares at prices quoted in euros or sterling. Investors could trade in euros if they chose, even though the shares themselves were still denominated in sterling. The two trading books would be independent and there would be no interaction between the two. The Stock Exchange would leave it to market forces to ensure that the two books were kept in line.

Broad support was expressed for the Exchange's proposals to enable companies to list and raise capital in euros from January 4, 1999. All price quotes for securities from euro-zone countries on SEAQ (the Stock Exchange's automated quotation system) will also be priced in euros from that date.

Response to the idea of dual trading was mixed and the Exchange's proposals now cater for a switch from sterling to euro order books on a stock by stock basis or *en masse* at any time after January 4, 1999, if the Exchange decides that the necessary criteria have been met. These criteria focus on the extent to which companies redenominate or investors wish to trade and settle in the euro. While quoted prices for U.K. securities denominated in sterling continue in sterling, demand for trading and settlement in euro will be met by currency conversion facilities from participants. The Exchange does not foresee a need to make substantive changes to the Listing Rules to accommodate companies that wish to convert their share capital to euros or to issue new shares in euros.

The London Stock Exchange and Deutsche Börse (Frankfurt) announced in July 1998 that they intend to harmonise the markets for their leading securities and to develop a joint electronic trading system. The aim is to create the nucleus of a single European stock market. The two exchanges have said that they would welcome the participation of other exchanges. If others participate, a pan-European market for some 300 blue chip equities is expected to develop. **4.04**

CREST (the electronic transfer and settlement system) has also announced its proposals.[3] Briefly, CREST already enables transactions to be settled in sterling or US dollars and this multi-currency facility will be extended to include the euro. Settlement in euros will be possible from January 1999. As the Republic of Ireland is to join the euro, Irish equities will be priced, traded, matched and settled in euros from January 1999.

FTSE International has indicated that U.K. indices such as the FTSE 100 will be based on companies domiciled in the U.K. for tax purposes, irrespective of the currency in which their share price is quoted or their shares are denominated. U.K. indices are expected to continue to be calculated in sterling until the majority of U.K. companies are trading in euros or the U.K. joins the euro area.

The derivatives markets are expected to reflect changes in the equity markets. So, individual stock options are likely to move to euro quotations at the same time as the underlying stock itself changes to being quoted in the euro. The strike price is expected to be converted at the relevant exchange rate on the day that the underlying stock converts to the euro.

Why would a company wish voluntarily to redenominate its shares to the euro?

Why would a U.K. company wish to redenominate its share capital into euros earlier than legally necessary? There are several possible reasons: **4.05**

(a) Companies may wish to raise equity finance in the new euro equity markets if this proves to be an attractive source of funds.

(b) If companies have substantial euro earnings, they may want to match their capital base against those euro earnings.

(c) If companies convert their balance sheets into euros, they may wish to convert their share capital at the same time.

---

[3] "CREST and EMU" issued by CREST Co. Ltd, February 1998.

(d) Companies may decide to convert to euros to reflect their status as European businesses, particularly if they have large business operations inside the euro area.

(e) Companies may have to be responsive to the wishes of investors who want the flexibility of investing in euro shares or sterling shares (or both) and may also wish to enhance their appeal to investors inside the euro area.

4.06   If they issue new shares in euros, companies may decide to redenominate existing shares into euro at the same time unless they are content to have dual currency share capital.

It is primarily the largest companies which are most likely to be interested in early redenomination. There are currently 2,683 companies listed on the London Stock Exchange's main market — 526 of which are foreign companies. Some 36 per cent of Europe's top 300 companies by market capitalisation are U.K. listed companies. Many of them have substantial businesses within the euro area, as well as secondary listings on other stock exchanges in Europe. In contrast, many private companies may decide to wait. Approximately 88 per cent out of the 1.25 million companies on the U.K. register at March 31, 1997, had issued share capital of less than £1,000.

Timing of Redenomination — what is the choice?

4.07   The main question for a U.K. company is when to redenominate its share capital. Broadly, there are three choices:

(a) First, it may redenominate its shares into euro while the U.K. is outside the euro area, recognising that the exchange rate between sterling and the euro will fluctuate from day to day.

(b) Second, it may wait until the U.K. decides whether to join the euro area and, if it does join, to redenominate during the transition period for the UK's entry, by which time an irrevocably fixed conversion rate between sterling and the euro will have been announced.

(c) Third, it may wait until the end of the U.K. transition period, when all references to sterling are expected to be automatically read under the relevant Council Regulation as references to euros at the fixed conversion rate.

It is not easy to predict how many companies will wish to redenominate in advance of the U.K. deciding whether to join, since many companies are currently adopting a "wait and see" approach. Much may depend on how quickly and widely the euro is adopted by businesses and (in the case of public listed companies) on how investor demand develops and the equity markets respond. It is possible that more companies will decide to redenominate their shares than plan to do so at the moment. In addition, companies which are subsidiaries of holding companies incorporated within the euro area may wish to redenominate their share capital into euros if their holding companies do so.

If the U.K. decides to join, a substantial increase is expected in the number of companies choosing to redenominate voluntarily, mainly amongst the larger company sector. The majority of small to medium sized companies may leave redenomination until the end of the transitional period.

Impact on U.K. companies — what is the position while the U.K. is "out"?

Where existing shares are denominated in a currency which is not being replaced by the euro, the relevant company will be unaffected. So, if shares are denominated in sterling or US dollars, they will continue in that currency. A company will be able, after January 1, 1999, to issue new shares in euro units as a matter of existing English company law[4] if it chooses to do so, whether the U.K. is "in" or "out".

4.08

Currently Sections 117 and 118 of the Companies Act 1985 require that the nominal or par value of the issued share capital of a U.K. registered public company will be £50,000 or such other sum as may be specified by statutory instrument. This requirement was introduced to implement Article 6 of the E.C. Second Company Law Directive[5] which requires that a public company will on incorporation have a minimum subscribed capital of not less than 25,000 ECU. As the ECU will be replaced by the euro on January 1, 1999 for the purposes of Community legislation, including the Second Company Law Directive, the DTI takes the view that this will permit any E.U. member state to lay down a minimum capital requirement expressed in euro, as well as an amount expressed in its national currency.

If a company has shares denominated in a participating national currency unit such as French Francs, those shares will continue to be denominated in that national currency unit during the transition period (from January 1, 1999 to December 31, 2001), unless redenominated by the company into euro voluntarily. This results from the "no compulsion" principle in Article 8(1) of the Second Regulation.[6] If a company does not voluntarily redenominate, dividends and other amounts will be treated as payable on the shares in euros at the fixed conversion rate from the end of the transition period. Although this Regulation will not apply directly to the U.K. while it is out, monetary provisions in the Regulation are expected to be recognised by an English court under the principles of private international law.

If shares are redenominated to the euro, will the rounding rule apply?

There has been debate on the question of how share capital will be converted and whether it will be rounded. The rounding of share capital and the par values of individual shares would result in an increase or reduction of a

4.09

---

[4] Re Scandinavian Bank Group plc [1987] 2 All E.R. 70.
[5] Directive 77/91 EEC of December 13, 1976
[6] Council Regulation (E.C.) No. 974/98 of May 3, 1998.

company's share capital, which could lead to legal complications. This needs to be avoided, particularly where redenomination occurs automatically at the end of the transition period (as contemplated in Article 14 of the second Regulation). Conversion to an unrounded amount would not have this result. It would lead to the par value of a share being stated (after conversion) to several decimal places, but this should not be a practical problem, since nominal share values have little or no impact on trading and settlement. The key factor is that there should be no alteration to the number of shares in issue.

A potential source of confusion is that rounding is capable of being used in at least three different senses with different results. The first type of rounding is mandatory rounding under Article 5 of the first Regulation, which applies when a monetary amount after conversion into euro is to be "paid or accounted for". The primary purpose of Article 5 is to establish precisely how much is to be paid or otherwise satisfied in order to discharge a debt after its conversion into euros. Much turns on what is meant by "paid or accounted for". It is suggested that this should not be given too wide an interpretation because this might otherwise have a greater effect than intended on the relationship between the parties to a legal instrument. In particular, "accounted for" should be interpreted in the narrower legal sense: an example is where two parties bring into account several items for the purpose of achieving a net settlement. Although there are differing views on the question, it is suggested that total share capital should not be treated, for Article 5 purposes, as being "accounted for" in this sense merely because it appears in the company's balance sheet.

4.10   The second type of rounding is voluntary rounding, where, for instance, a company in general meeting voluntarily decides to round or renominalise the par value of its shares and/or increase or reduce the amount of its share capital with the requisite approval of its shareholders.

The third type of rounding is presentational rounding, where monetary amounts in euros are rounded to convenient figures for information purposes only, without any intention to alter the relevant amount for legal purposes. For example, where a U.K. public company reports its financial results to the London Stock Exchange and the press, it is common to round the figures (including the amount of its share capital and reserves) to the nearest thousand pounds. This is well understood by investors and indeed is normally clear from the financial statement itself. In principle, there appears to be no reason why companies should not be able to state euro amounts in round figures for information purposes to the same extent that they can do so now. Where a company uses rounding for presentational reasons, this should be made clear in order to avoid any confusion. This ought not to be a practical problem in cases where rounding is already permitted.

4.11   It is suggested that, on this analysis, both the total amount of share capital and the par value of each share should be converted into euro under Article 4 of the First Regulation and that, for this purpose, mandatory rounding would not apply. This would avoid an increase or reduction in share capital and any mismatch (after conversion) between total share capital and the sum of the par values. As recognised above, the total share capital and par values would be stated to several decimal places. However, companies would be free to renominalise their shares or (where permitted by domestic law) convert to shares of no par value if they chose to do so, subject to obtaining the necessary authorisation. They would also be free to state their share capital in round figures for information purposes, provided that it was clear this was being done. Whatever analysis it may finally adopt, the European Commission is expected to permit the above result in the case of share capital redenomination, since it has already stated that the rounding rule requires only a minimum standard of accuracy and does not prevent the use of a greater number of decimal places.

The mandatory rounding rule would come into play only when a monetary amount is to be "paid or accounted for" after conversion. So, for instance, if a dividend was payable or capital was to be returned to shareholders, then mandatory rounding would apply to the amount to be paid. Presumably it is intended that mandatory rounding should apply to the total amount payable to each shareholder and not to the amount referable to each individual share. If the dividend on each share were to be rounded, this would lead to a significant increase or reduction in the total amount payable.

Need for a simplified procedure for redenominating existing shares

The introduction of the euro will have its greatest impact on existing share capital. The difficulty is that the Companies Act 1985 does not at present provide a specific and inexpensive procedure for redenominating shares in a different currency. If a company wished to redenominate existing shares into euro, this could be done, for instance, by cancelling the existing shares and issuing new euro shares, but any reorganisation of share capital that involved the cancellation of existing shares would (subject to limited exceptions) require both court and shareholder approval under current law. This is not a practical solution. A court application could be avoided by using the powers conferred on a company by Chapter VII of the Companies Act 1985 to purchase its own shares and then to issue new shares. Again, this procedure is likely to be too cumbersome and costly to be used widely. A simplified procedure for redenominating shares in any currency needs to be introduced to avoid these complications.

4.12

If companies redenominate shares into euro, conversion would invariably result in the par values of those shares being restated to several decimal places. Companies might well choose to reorganise the affected shares in order to achieve round par values. This is more likely in Member States, such as the U.K., where shares with relatively small par values are common.

A company is able to consolidate and/or sub-divide its shares if authorised by its articles of association, although this power can be exercised by the company only in general meeting.[7] It might be more difficult to produce shares with a round nominal amount by consolidation and sub-division than was the case with U.K. decimalisation in 1971. An alternative method might be for a

4.13

---

[7] Section 121(2)(b) of the Companies Act 1985.

company to convert its paid-up shares into stock and reconvert that stock into paid-up shares of different denominations, assuming that the company was authorised to do so by its articles of association. Again, this power would be exercisable only by the company in general meeting. As this power is rarely used, it is no longer a standard provision in modern articles of association. It would also be necessary to deal with any fractional interests arising on reconversion. For instance, this might involve selling the fractional interests and distributing the cash proceeds to shareholders. The "cashing out" of fractional entitlements could have tax implications.

The DTI invited comments on these questions in its consultation document issued in January 1998 and is currently considering the responses received.[8]

No par value shares — a solution?

4.14   One method of avoiding many of these difficulties is to introduce no par value shares into English company law, as recommended by successive company law reform committees.[9] If companies are permitted (at their option) to convert their share capital wholly into shares of no par value in any currency (including euro), this would reduce the problems which would otherwise arise when shares are redenominated. The number of shares in issue could remain the same; there would be no par value to redenominate; no resulting decimal figures to round or renominalise; and changes to registers and certificates would be minimal. It would also avoid the need to deal with any awkward fractional interests which may arise when shares are redenominated and renominalised.

It was recommended by the above committees that a company should be able to convert its share capital wholly to shares without par value by a special resolution. A company with a share capital of £1,000 divided into 1,000 shares of £1 each (before conversion) would have a share capital of £1,000 divided simply into 1,000 shares (after conversion). Each shareholder would continue to have the same proportionate interest in the company: so, a holder of 100 shares of £1 each (before conversion) would continue to have a 10 per cent stake in the company. Each share certificate would state the number of shares which it represented, the number of shares which the company was authorised to issue and, where the shares were partly paid, the amount paid on each share. The total amount of paid up share capital, together with any amount on share premium account, would be transferred to a stated capital account. New issue proceeds would be credited to the same account, as would transfers from profits or reserves made by special resolution.

Additional benefits of no par value shares

4.15   If introduced into English company law, a system of "true" no par value shares would offer not only the opportunity for companies to side step the

---

[8] "The Euro: Redenomination of Share Capital — A Consultative Document", DTI, January 1998.
[9] See the Report of the Gedge Committee on Shares of No Par Value (1954); the Report of the Jenkins Committee on Company Law Reform (1962); and the Report of the Wilson Committee on Financial Institutions (1980).

need to renominalise shares after conversion to euro but also additional benefits (which might still be attractive to a company even if it decided not to redenominate its shares into euro):

(a) It represents the share for what it is — a fraction of the equity. It would avoid the complication and confusion that can result from giving a share a fixed nominal value which is unconnected with its true market value.

(b) The concept of par value is a historic concept which has largely lost its significance in terms of providing a pool of permanent capital for the protection of creditors and shareholders. Public companies invariably issue shares by reference to their market value which will usually be at or above par. With limited exceptions, an issue at a discount to par is prohibited by law but par no longer represents a meaningful measure of the permanent capital of a company.

(c) It would simplify the system of share capital maintenance by removing the distinction between the par value and the issue price of a share and also the largely artificial distinction between "nominal share capital" and "share premium". Subscription money would be treated simply as part of total share capital.

(d) It would give greater flexibility in arranging a company's capital structure. So, if a share is trading at a disproportionately high price, the shares can be easily split into a larger number of shares to improve their marketability without the artificial limit imposed by a par value.

(e) If the market price falls below the issue price, a company can raise additional capital by issuing new no par value shares without being constrained by the rules against the issue of shares at a discount to par.

(f) It would enable London, as an international equity market, to offer a type of share familiar to investors in other major equity markets such as the USA (and Canada) and its simplicity would make it more intelligible to less sophisticated investors.

The adoption of a system of "true" no par value shares would involve consequential changes to existing legislation, such as the capital maintenance rules, and so would require detailed study. Although technical issues would arise, none of them should create any insurmountable on-going difficulty. One issue is whether there might be scope for confusion if a company were to be permitted to create a new class of no par value share but also to retain its existing par value shares. This potential problem could be avoided by stipulating that a company could not have a share capital consisting partly of shares having par value and partly of shares without par value.[10] In other words, if a company wanted no par value shares, it would have to convert wholly to this type of share.

4.16

Another issue is whether conversion of existing shares with a par value into shares of no par value might affect class rights. If a company has more than

---

[10] This was the conclusion reached by the Gedge Committee (paragraphs 41 and 72(4) of their Report).

one class of share, the class rights may be defined by reference to amounts paid up on those shares. Removal of the par value could constitute a variation of class rights. Hence it may be appropriate to provide that, where the shares of a company are divided into two or more classes, the sanction of holders of each class of share in separate meetings is necessary if those shares are to be converted into shares of no par value. It is also suggested that the use of no par value shares should be optional and not compulsory.[11]

E.C. Second Company Law Directive — a constraint?

4.17   A key factor is that public companies would at present need to act within the framework laid down by the 1976 Second Company Law Directive (which applies to public limited companies) if English company law is changed to permit no par value shares. The Directive is linked to a system of no par value shares which, in its then existing form, was rejected as an unsatisfactory "halfway house" by the Gedge Committee Report in 1954. In particular, the Directive contemplates that, although shares may be issued without a par value, they will have an "accountable par". This concept is not defined in the Directive. It is based on the Belgian type of no par value share which evolved in the 1870s, although it was only recognised by legislation in 1913.

The "accountable par" variant is more restrictive, as it applies the principle of parity. This is understood to operate as follows. Assuming an issue of 1,000 shares of BFr 500 per share, the "accountable par" is BFr 500. If a subsequent issue is made at a higher price, the "accountable par" is automatically raised to a figure equal to the total amount in the capital account (less reserves), divided by the numbers of shares in issue. The premium paid on the new shares is credited to a reserve. New shares may not be issued at a price less than "accountable par". Without this principle of parity, questions of discount and premium would not arise.

The Directive does not deal with the possibility that new shares might have to be issued at a price lower than "accountable par" because of a change in market conditions. In addition, where the Directive refers, in its capital maintenance, reserve, reduction, redemption provisions, to the nominal value of a share, it includes a reference to its "accountable par" if it has no nominal value. As a result, "accountable par" appears to be treated for many purposes in a similar way to par value. This more restricted form of no par value share is probably sufficient to reduce the problem of achieving round par values when shares are converted into euros. (Indeed, it is essentially this system which, it appears, is being considered by Austria, France and Germany). The concern in the U.K. is that the concept of "accountable par" would be a complicating factor and would reduce the other potential benefits otherwise available.

4.18   The adoption of the restricted variant would be a missed opportunity to gain the wider benefits offered by "true" no par value shares. In particular, the "accountable par" variant would have the following limitations:

---

[11] *cf.* the Australian Company Law Reform Bill 1997 which contains a provision for the compulsory use of no par value shares.

(a) it would not simplify the capital maintenance rules and would appear to perpetuate (through the concept of "accountable par") many of the artificial distinctions and limits associated with par values;

(b) it could create an artificial "floor" for the price below which new shares could not be issued and might restrict flexibility in arranging or altering a company's capital structure;

(c) it would involve substantial amendments to the Companies Act and the Accountancy Standards in return for marginal benefits and might also cause fresh complication rather than avoid it.

Consequently, it is debateable whether this restricted system of no par value share offers a significantly better solution than other available options, such as making legislative changes to permit companies to redenominate and renominalise shares more easily. In contrast, a system of "true" no par value shares would be much more attractive to companies. Moves are being made to clarify with the European Commission whether the Directive does have a limiting effect and, if so, to discuss ways to permit the introduction of "true" no par value shares in those member states that wish to adopt this system.

What conversion rate should apply if a U.K. company redenominates its shares to the euro?

One question raised by the DTI in its consultation paper is whether legislation should prescribe how companies fix the conversion rate that will be used to redenominate shares into euro while the U.K. is "out". The DTI asked for comments whether legislation should specify a particular day on which the conversion rate would be determined and, if so, what date this should be. **4.19**

There appears to be general support for making the legislation as flexible as possible. Although a company should not be free to select any conversion rate that it may think fit, it seems sensible to permit a company to fix:

(a) the conversion rate at a particular time which is not more than, say, 14 days prior to the despatch of the notice of meeting to shareholders; or

(b) the conversion rate at a specified time on the date on which the redenomination is to take effect; or

(c) an average of the exchange rates at a specified time over a number of consecutive business days.

The legislation should permit companies to use whichever method they believe is most appropriate. In practice, companies may well wish to use a method which determines the conversion rate in advance of the meeting, so that the impact of redenomination can be properly judged and steps taken to renominalise shares where necessary to achieve round par values. **4.20**

Another question is who should authorise the redenomination of existing shares — the directors or the shareholders? While the U.K. is out and there is a fluctuating exchange rate between sterling and the euro, it seems appropriate for a share redenomination to require at least an ordinary resolution of shareholders. This would be important for shareholder protection. However, if the U.K. joins and the conversion rate between sterling and the euro becomes irrevocably locked, there may be a case for permitting redenomination by a directors' resolution. This may save costs without exposing shareholders to an exchange rate risk. A similar procedure already exists under the Uncertificated Securities Regulations 1995 which enables the directors of a company to dematerialise its shares for transfer in CREST, subject to shareholders having the right by an ordinary resolution to reverse the directors' resolution if they object.

What forward planning issues should be considered?

4.21   Forward planning is essential. Even if a company adopts a "wait and see" approach to share redenomination, it is sensible to think out the issues now and to plan ahead. A company may want to obtain shareholder authority in advance to issue euro shares if and when the directors decide. If a company in an "out" country goes further and redenominates voluntarily, it must decide on the exchange rate to be used as indicated above. In addition, the costs of even a simple mailing to shareholders by a major public company can be substantial. Practical difficulties would occur if a large number of companies attempted to hold general meetings over a short period of time. These costs and difficulties could be reduced if a company was able to plan in advance to table the necessary members' resolutions at the next Annual General Meeting rather than holding an Extraordinary General Meeting.

Whether or not it decides to redenominate, a company may wish to consider giving its shareholders a choice of the currency in which to receive dividends. If a share is denominated in sterling, the shareholder may still be given a right (if the company's articles of association are sufficiently flexible) to elect whether to receive dividend payments in sterling or euro. A company will also need to decide when to convert its accounts into euro, as it may wish to redenominate its share capital at the same time. In addition, if a company has preference shares, convertibles, options or warrants, it will need to consider how these will be affected by redenomination and what changes may be necessary. These issues need to be identified and addressed in good time.

ADDENDUM

Legislative proposals on share capital redenomination

Since the rest of this chapter was prepared, the Department of Trade and Industry (DTI) has announced its plans to introduce a simplified statutory procedure enabling U.K. companies more easily to redenominate their share capital to any currency (including the euro) and to permit a public company to maintain its minimum share capital in a currency other than sterling if it chooses. A summary of the proposals is set out below.

Lord Simon, the Minister for Trade and Competitiveness in Europe, announced on September 25, 1998, new legislation to introduce a simplified procedure to enable U.K. companies to redenominate their share capital to the euro (or any other currency) and to permit a public company to maintain its minimum allotted share capital in a currency other than sterling. The changes are being proposed to help U.K. business prepare for the euro in response to submissions received to the consultation document issued by the DTI in January 1998.

The following framework of statutory rules on redenomination is proposed:

- Companies would be permitted to resolve that references in any document to share capital denominated in one currency would be read as a reference to the equivalent amount in the euro (or another currency). A resolution of each class of shareholders would be required. However, a directors' resolution would suffice where the company was redenominating its shares into euro during any U.K. transitional period to membership of the euro, subject to a shareholders' power of veto.

- Permitted methods would be prescribed for fixing the exchange rate to be used when converting share capital to a different currency. This would be particularly relevant while there is a fluctuating exchange rate between the euro and sterling. Companies would, for example, have a choice of the rate prevailing on any day within a specified period in advance of the conversion day, or an average over a period.

- Companies would be required to adopt a top-down method of conversion, by converting at the level of total nominal amount of each class of shares (rather than at the level of each individual share) and rounding that amount to the nearest legal unit or sub-unit of the currency concerned. This minor rounding would not trigger any requirement for court or shareholder approval. Companies would derive individual par values by dividing converted share capital by the number of shares in issue, leaving that figure stated to several decimal places if they so wish.

- Companies would be permitted to adjust the resulting par value of each share to a more convenient round figure in euro (or other currency), subject to shareholder approval but without the need for court approval. There would be no requirement for companies to issue new share certificates following redenomination. Any change in the total nominal share capital would be combined with a corresponding adjustment to the company's reserves.

Where shareholders or third parties have rights which are linked to the par value of the share, it is expected that companies would not be able to use the new procedure in a way which would alter those rights, without the consent of all those concerned.

The new legislation will not deal with no par value shares. The DTI recognises that there is strong support for the introduction of a system of U.S. style, "true" no par value shares. However, the European Commission has confirmed to the DTI that the E.C. Second Company Law Directive would not currently permit this kind of arrangement. Any changes to the Second Directive would require the agreement of other Member States, as well as a formal proposal from the Commission. The company law review being carried out by the DTI is considering the wider issue of reform of the capital maintenance rules as a priority.

The proposals to amend the Companies Act 1985 will be put forward using powers available under the Deregulation and Contracting Out Act 1994. A further consultation document is to be issued by the DTI in early 1999 and the changes could be inplace by the end of 1999.

5

Financial Contracts and Instruments

by Dina Albagli, Herbert Smith

The issues arising out of EMU affect a great number of contractual obligations but perhaps give rise to the most sensitive concerns in the context of financial contracts and instruments, including loan agreements, debt securities (whether in the form of notes, bonds or otherwise) and derivative contracts. The analysis of the issues follows these three broad categories.

5.01

Loan Agreements

Continuity of contract

The over-arching issue of continuity of contract has been discussed in Chapter 2, along with the provisions of Council Regulation (E.C.) No. 1103/97 (the "First Regulation") which seek to address these issues. Loan agreements are affected in the same manner as any other contract which requires payment in a participating currency. The fundamental position under English law is that, unless the parties have specifically agreed otherwise, the introduction of the euro will not give a party the right unilaterally to terminate the contract, frustrate the contract or excuse performance under the contract.[1] Continuity language is therefore not generally included in loan agreements.

  The First Regulation is not applicable in jurisdictions outside the E.U. and as a result the legal position has also been clarified in certain U.S. states namely

5.02

---

[1] See Financial Law Panel — Economic and Monetary Union — Continuity of Contracts in English Law — January 1998 where the FLP expresses the view that EMU would not call into question the continuity of financial contracts. Issues which they identified relating to the disappearance of price sources and ECU debt are dealt with below. The FLP has also produced reports in relation to continuity of contracts in a number of key jurisdictions such as Switzerland, Singapore and Japan.

the state of New York, California and Illinois. It is being considered in other U.S. states and other jurisdictions (such as Hong Kong).

Loans denominated in participating currencies

5.03   The mechanism by which payment obligations expressed in the original currency are translated into the new currency are clear, albeit somewhat complex, during the Transitional Period. The stages of such translation of amounts in a loan agreement (in this example, Deutsche Marks) are likely to be the following:

5.04   (a) The original payment obligations (whether to repay the principal or to pay interest, fees or costs and expenses) will be expressed in Deutsche Marks. Often, the loan agreement will provide a definition along the lines of:

> " 'Deutsche Mark' and 'DM' means the lawful currency for the time being of the Federal Republic of Germany"

Thus an obligation to pay "Deutsche Marks" shall be an obligation to pay the lawful currency of Germany.

(b) The question "what is the currency of Germany?" is a matter which, under a widely recognised principle of private international law,[2] is decided by reference to German law. Thus English courts will look to German law to determine what a reference to Deutsche Marks or German currency means, even where the loan agreement is expressed to be governed by English law. German law in this instance will be Council Regulation (E.C.) No. 974/98 (the "Second Regulation"), being European Community legislation which is directly applicable within the participating Member States.

(c) On January 1, 1999, according to the Second Regulation, the euro will replace the Deutsche Mark as the lawful currency of Germany at the fixed conversion rate.[3] From then on, the payment obligation will be to pay the new lawful currency of Germany, *i.e.* euro.

(d) During the Transitional Period, the currency of the euro will exist as euro units and many different "national currency units", of which the Deutsche Mark will be one.[4] Thus the obligation to pay euro can be satisfied by paying the number of national currency units (in our example, 100 Deutsche Mark) stipulated in the original agreement.[5] If the parties agree for payment to be in euro units or the payer wishes to pay in euro units into a German bank account, which it is free to do,[6] the 100 Deutsche Mark will be converted into euro units at the fixed conversion rate, and rounded in accordance with the rounding rules.[7]

---

[2] The principle of *lex monetae* — See Dicey & Morris: *The Conflict of Laws* (12th Edition) and F.A. Mann: *The Legal Aspects of Money* (5th Edition).
[3] Articles 1 and 2, Second Regulation.
[4] Article 6, Second Regulation — See Chapter 2 above.
[5] Article 8(1), Second Regulation.
[6] See paragraph 5.09 below.
[7] Article 8(2) and (3), Second Regulation and Article 4(4), First Regulation.

(e) At the end of the Transitional Period (January 1, 2002), the reference in the loan agreement to "100 Deutsche Mark" will be replaced automatically by legislation by a reference to the equivalent amount in euro at the fixed conversion rate and rounded in accordance with the rounding rules.[8]

Where the loan agreement does not contain a currency definition, it is also unlikely that there will be much difficulty, provided that a court is able to determine which old currency the parties intended (difficulties, unrelated to EMU, could arise, for example, if a loan agreement referred solely to "franc" without specifying France, Switzerland, Belgium or Luxembourg). Once it is clear to which currency and country a loan agreement refers, an obligation to pay an amount denominated in that currency is an obligation to pay an amount of whatever units the laws of that country determine is that currency.

Even after January 1, 1999, it will still be valid to continue referring to Deutsche Marks in a loan document, particularly where the parties continue to wish for the loan to be recorded in Deutsche Marks or for the payment to be in Deutsche Mark units. For example, if the lender or, more likely, the borrower has not yet switched its accounting systems into euro, it may prefer to lend or borrow in Deutsche Mark units. As a matter of documentation, it would be preferable for parties to begin after January 1, 1999 to use a definition of "Deutsche Mark" which reflects that it is no longer a currency in its own right, but is a sub-division of the euro, which is the lawful currency of Germany, although the old-style definitions would generally continue to produce the result outlined above.

Loans denominated in Sterling (and other "out" currencies)

The above analysis of how payment obligations will be translated will probably apply to Sterling and the other European currencies which are not initial participants as and when these currencies join EMU. The replacement of Sterling by the euro will undoubtedly be expressed in a European regulation which will reflect to some extent the Second Regulation. Whether it will replicate the Second Regulation exactly, or whether some different mechanism for a Transitional Period will be adopted, is not yet known and will not be known until these Member States reach a firm decision to join. However, the broad principles of the provisions described above will, in all likelihood, apply to future participants. In the meantime, using the usual definition of Sterling as "the lawful currency for the time being of the United Kingdom" is the best approach and any translation into euro will occur as described above. Parties to Sterling denominated loans may wish to provide from now in their documents for the consequences of the replacement of Sterling by the euro, which they can achieve either by specific provisions in each relevant clause or by giving themselves now the flexibility to make appropriate amendments at a later date.

5.05

---

[8] Article 14, Second Regulation.

Loans denominated in ECU

"Closed basket" ECU and "open basket" or "official" ECU

5.06   The ECU behaves differently to national currencies because the ECU is not the currency of any country. It is a basket of the currencies of the majority of the Member States, weighted according to the sizes of their respective economies. It is created by European community legislation,[9] and is the unit of account used by the institutions of the European Union. It is also used by private parties in loan agreements (or other financial instruments) and is, in this context, a creature of contract between the parties: it does not represent the obligations of any central bank but is, in effect, a measure of value or payment.

The parties to a contract may, and in the past frequently did, specify exactly what they meant by "ECU", setting out which national currencies it consisted of and in what proportion. This type of clause is known as a "closed basket" clause.

Alternatively, the parties might have chosen to define the ECU for the purpose of their loan agreement as whatever was determined by the European Community institutions to be the ECU. As the European Community grew and the components of this "official ECU" changed, this type of "open basket" clause became more convenient and popular, as the parties wished to track the official ECU without having to amend their loan agreement each time the official ECU changed.

5–07   The official ECU will be replaced by the euro at a rate of one for one on January 1, 1999[10] — there will be no Transitional Period as with the national currencies. However, Article 2 of the First Regulation does not provide that all references to the ECU are replaced by references to the euro — only the ECU "as referred to in Article 109(g) of the Treaty and as defined in Regulation (E.C.) No. 3320/94", *i.e.* the "official" ECU. It does, however, create a presumption, which is rebuttable, that references to the ECU in legal instruments shall be presumed to be references to the "official" ECU, unless the parties intended otherwise. Thus whether or not a reference to the ECU in a private loan document is translated to euro will depend on the construction of the contract. Although this clarifies the position within Member States, where the First Regulation will have effect, this does not necessarily mean that every reference in every document under any other governing law will automatically be converted to euro — the *lex monetae* principle of international law strictly only applies to currencies, not units of value such as the ECU. It is, therefore, a matter of the governing law of the contract to determine how a reference to ECU obligations should be dealt with,[11] although it can be expected that many legal systems would have regard to European Community law to help them in determining the matter. Therefore, a likely result is that where the ECU is specifically defined so as not to follow the official ECU (for example, with a "closed basket" clause) it will not convert to the euro; however where it is

---

[9] Regulation (E.C.) No. 3320/94.
[10] Article 2, First Regulation.
[11] For an analysis of the nature of the basket ECU, see Financial Law Panel — Economic and Monetary Union — Continuity of Contracts in English Law — January 1998.

defined so as to follow the official ECU, or where there is no definition at all
and the presumption is not rebutted, the reference to the ECU shall be replaced
by the euro and, if that is the case, any argument that the contract is frustrated
by reason of impossibility will, therefore, be precluded.

Economic consequences of conversion

A loan which was denominated in ECU might behave significantly differently   **5.08**
if it is converted into euro. The ECU moves as a measure of value reflecting a
basket of currencies, each with its own monetary authority. The euro will be a
new currency in its own right with a single system of monetary authorities.
Furthermore, the 12 currencies which make up the final composition of the
ECU are not the same as the 11 currencies which are initial participants in the
euro (Sterling, the Danish krone and the Greek drachma are comprised within
the ECU basket but not in EMU, the Finnish markka and Austrian schilling are
not in the ECU but will be in EMU). Monetary policy for the euro may differ
from the monetary policies of the currencies which made up the ECU and this,
along with market perceptions of the "hardness" or "softness" of the euro and
its new and untested central bank may affect the external value of the euro
compared to that which might have been expected of the ECU.

   As a result, a party may seek to argue that the commercial rationale of its
contract originally denominated in ECU had fundamentally changed, thereby
frustrating the contract. The purpose of the First Regulation is to preclude this
argument. In any event, it is also relevant to note that the possible replacement
of the ECU by the euro has been known for a long time, including the fact that
it would be replaced at a rate of one for one. Parties who do not wish to see
their ECU contractual obligations continue should, therefore, take steps to
terminate them.

Payments during the Transitional Period

Article 8 of the Second Regulation deals with how payments may be made   **5.09**
during the Transitional Period, when payments will be capable of being made
through the banking system (scriptural money) in both euro units and national
currency units, although only national currency notes and coins (fiduciary
money) will be in circulation. The basic rule is that obligations which are
denominated in a national currency unit continue to be payable in that national
currency unit. This is often referred to as the "no compulsion/no prohibition"
principle. Thus interest payments on a Deutsche Mark loan will continue to be
payable in Deutsche Marks (as "national currency units" of the euro) after
January 1, 1999. The parties are, however, free to agree for payments to be in
euro units instead. They also need to decide in which unit (or units) to record
drawings.

   There is a further significant exception to the payment rule:[12] an amount
denominated in the euro unit or a national currency unit and payable by
crediting an account within the Member State of that national currency can be
paid by the debtor either in the euro unit or in that national currency unit. The

---

[12] Article 8(3) Second Regulation.

institution receiving the payment is obliged to convert, if necessary, the incoming payment into the denomination of the account of the creditor. At the same time, that receiving institution does not need the authorisation of the account holder to make that conversion. The term "payable within that Member State" should not be interpreted as applying only to domestic payments, where both the account of the debtor and creditor are held in the same Member State. These provisions also apply to those cross border payments which are denominated in the euro unit or the national currency unit of the account of the creditor, provided that in the latter case such account is denominated in the national currency unit of the Member State where the account is located.[13]

The chart below illustrates when it is possible to make a payment in the currency unit other than the one specified. In practice, from January 1, 1999, wholesale interbank markets will deal only in the euro and banks will provide customers with facilities to deal in national currency units if required.

	Euro account[14] in Germany	Euro account[14] in France	DM account[14] in Germany	DM account[14] in France	FF account[14] in Germany	FF account[14] in France
Debt in euro	Yes — art. 8(1) applies. No conversion necessary	Yes — art. 8(1) applies. No conversion necessary	Yes — art. 8(3) applies. Payee's bank will convert	No — not "within that Member State"	No — not "within that Member State"	Yes — art. 8(3) applies. Payee's bank will convert
Debt in DM	Yes — art. 8(3) applies. Payee's bank will convert	No — not "within that Member State"	Yes — art. 8(1) applies. No conversion necessary	Yes — art. 8(1) applies. No conversion necessary	No — art. 8(3) does not apply	No — not "within that Member State"
Debt in FF	No — not "within that Member State"	Yes — art. 8(3) applies. Payee's bank will convert	No — not "within that Member State"	No — art. 8(3) does not apply	Yes — art. 8(1) applies. No conversion necessary	Yes — art. 8(1) applies. No conversion necessary

5.10   Where the institution receiving the payment is obliged in the circumstances described above to convert the incoming payment into the denomination of the account of the creditor, it will find itself bearing any costs of such conversion. To avoid these costs in the context of amounts lent, some banks are requiring

---

[13] Recital 13 Second Regulation.
[14] Reference to the account here is to the account of the creditor. The same result applies so long as the account of the debtor is in a Member State, whether or not the same Member State as that of the creditor's account.

the borrower, in the terms of their loan, to make payments during the Transitional Period in the euro unit only , effectively circumventing by agreement the "no compulsion" principle. The borrower should consider whether it is prepared to accept such a restriction.

Payments at the end of the Transitional Period

At the end of the Transitional Period, the euro will cease to be denominated in national currency units as well as in euro units; the only scriptural money will be the euro and fiduciary money in the form of national currency units will cease to be used at the latest six months after the end of that period.

5.11

Fixed and Floating Rate Loans — Economic consequences of conversion

Fixed Rate Loans

The conversion of a fixed rate loan from a national currency to the euro, according to the mechanisms set out above, is fairly unproblematic. However, the economic impact of some fixed rate loans converting into euro may be significant, particularly where the loan has been set at a fixed rate over a very long period.

5.12

The reason for this is that the fixed rate of interest may have been calculated to reflect the anticipated movements of national currency interest rates; for example, the Deutsche Mark, which has historically, in the post-war period, been a stable currency with generally low interest rates. A loan with such a fixed rate may become significantly more or less expensive compared to the new euro interest rates after EMU, given that euro interest rates will be set to reflect the whole euro zone economy rather than just one Member State's. If euro rates are higher than the old Deutsche Mark rates, a lender would have an incentive to seek to terminate the original loan in order to recover his money and re-lend it at the new higher rates and, conversely if euro rates are lower than the old Deutsche Mark rates, a borrower would have an incentive to seek to terminate the original loan and get a new and cheaper loan in the market.

Clearly the mere fact that interest rates change does not affect the validity of the loan agreement; fixed rate loans are designed to deal with a background of floating market rates, and their pricing will reflect market expectations of future movements in floating rates. The potential problem arising on EMU is that the entire set of assumptions on which that pricing was based may no longer be true. The fact that this is accompanied by, and results from what is clearly, a major change in the economies of the countries concerned might encourage a party to test the continuity of contract provisions contained in the First Regulation.

5.13

One argument which has been mooted, but to some extent discounted,[15] is that such a frustrating event arises from the economic consequences of EMU

---

[15] See the Financial Law Panel: Economic and Monetary Union — Continuity of Contracts — October 1996 and Economic and Monetary Union — Continuity of Contracts in English Law — January 1998.

(*i.e.* the change in overall interest rates) rather than the introduction of the euro itself. The continuity of contract provision in the First Regulation speaks only about the introduction of the euro and not its economic consequences.

The chances of such arguments succeeding are however thought to be slim, barring some catastrophic economic consequences of EMU where there really might be a valid reason for parties to be able to invoke force majeure clauses or to claim that contracts have been frustrated. Whether such loan agreements could really be challenged would also depend to a large extent on when the loan agreement was entered into and for what length of time. The possibility of EMU has been known to the financial and business community for a very long time and, as the likelihood of it actually occurring has increased, its potential impact has been factored more and more into the pricing of financial instruments. It would, therefore, be fairly difficult for a party to show that it was completely unaware of the possibility of EMU at the time of entering into a loan agreement any time since the date of the Maastricht Treaty.

Floating Rate Loans

5.14   The rate of interest payable under a floating rate loan might vary in a manner beyond the expectations of the parties when they initially entered into the loan, if the new euro interest rates were to behave significantly differently from the interest rates for the old national currency in which the loan was taken out. There would not be the same market incentive as with fixed rate loans to go out into the market and refinance the loan at a better rate, and a party seeking to invoke a force majeure clause or claiming frustration of the contract would be facing even more difficulties than those outlined above in relation to fixed rate loans, as he would have to show that the change was not within his expectation, despite the known volatility of interest rates.

Price Sources — disappearance and replacement

5.15   A separate issue does, however, arise in relation to floating rate loans. Depending on how the loan agreement is drafted and how the parties have designated the floating rate which will apply, the parties may find it difficult to ascertain, after the occurrence of EMU, what is the floating rate which applies to their loan agreement.

Bank's base rate

5.16   References to a specific bank's base rate for deposits in a specific currency are unlikely to cause any difficulty as the replacement of that currency by the euro will result in the reference becoming a reference to that bank's base rate for deposits in euro.

Reference Bank rate

5.17   Where a loan agreement refers to the base rates of a panel of "Reference Banks", the same issues as above will apply in relation to each Reference Bank and little difficulty should arise. A further element however is the criteria for selection of a Reference Bank: many loan agreements will refer to "prime banks in the London interbank market" (or Frankfurt or Paris as the case may be). The potential difficulty is that the concept of the city-based financial centre is likely, over time, to lose its significance within the euro zone. Thus it may become irrelevant that a certain bank is situated in Paris or Frankfurt when it comes to its suitability to be a Reference Bank. The concept of the London interbank market will survive for some time, at least until Sterling participates in EMU, but in relation to London the issue arises as to whether loans in European currencies should be set by reference to the London interbank market rather than the new euro zone market.

Price sponsor's rate
It is also common, particularly in wholesale money market transactions, for interest rates to be calculated by reference to the cost of borrowing in the interbank market of a particular financial centre. Examples are LIBOR (London Interbank Offered Rate), PIBOR (Paris Interbank Offered Rate) and FIBOR (Frankfurt Interbank Offered Rate), which are set by various price sponsors and are frequently designated by the name of the currency, the price sponsor and the page number of a screen provider, such as Dow Jones Telerate, on which the rate appears. Most of these price sponsors (the sponsor of the most widely used LIBOR rates is the British Bankers' Association) have indicated that they will designate officially formal replacement rates when the old rates disappear because the currencies to which they relate no longer exist. Many have also indicated how they will designate the new rates, either displaying the new rate on the same page as the old rate or referring to a new page number.

    It is believed that under the laws of most E.U. Member States the disappearance of a price source will not affect continuity of legacy contracts (*i.e.* contracts already in place at the beginning of the Transitional Period), even where there is no agreed fallback in the contract. In the absence of such a fallback it would appear that the courts would substitute a suitable successor rate. Certain courts are likely, upon the disappearance of a rate such as PIBOR, to provide for the rate to be determined by quotations from leading banks in, in this case, the Paris interbank market. The difficulty with this fallback is that it will place an enormous strain on the institution required to obtain these quotes and also on the leading banks required to provide them. Furthermore, it is not necessarily appropriate for reference banks to determine such a rate in view of the existence of EURIBOR. It is arguable that that is the appropriate successor to, for instance, PIBOR, as EURIBOR will be the representative rate for the whole euro zone. On the other hand, it could be argued that the EURIBOR rate is substantially different from the PIBOR rate, as EURIBOR is determined on the basis of a much larger panel of banks and spans a wider geographical area and is not, therefore, really a direct successor to PIBOR. It is probable that different courts in Member States will approach this issue differently, those taking a literal interpretation of the contract preferring the reference bank fallback and those agreeing to a more conceptual approach preferring the EURIBOR fallback. A similar problem arises in respect of overnight notes which will be replaced by the new EONIA in the eurozone and Euronia in the London market.

5.18

5.19   This uncertainty is unwelcome in the markets both in respect of legacy and new contracts and legislative and contractual solutions have been and are being considered.

A number of Member States are passing legislation naming EURIBOR as the relevant successor to their interbank offered rate. Those which have not are being pressed to clarify whether EURIBOR will replace their local rate or not. The relevant legislation would only cover contracts governed by the law of the country passing such legislation; for instance, French legislation will apply to French law contracts referring to PIBOR and not English law contracts referring to PIBOR; equally, the French legislation will not deal with contracts referring to, for example, the Madrid interbank offered rate. The fact that some price sponsors will designate official replacement rates and will display them on the same page will also assist greatly in the use of legacy contracts. However, there remain situations where contractual measures to achieve the most appropriate position will be necessary. These instances are more likely to arise in the context of derivatives[16] than in loan agreements.

Market Conventions

5.20   The introduction of the euro and the disappearance of 11 national currencies has necessitated the harmonisation of market conventions applying to trading and settlement of not only the euro money markets but also the bond and foreign exchange markets. Currently, each financial centre in Europe is identified with a particular currency and market conventions in the money market are clearly linked to the financial centre of the currency. Lack of harmonisation would cause great confusion and potential for mistakes would arise.

The European Commission, the EMI and the Member States have generally decided to leave the market to sort this problem out. The leading international trade associations, namely IPMA, IBMA, ISDA, the Association Cambiste Internationale, the International Paying Agents Association, Cedel Bank and Morgan Guaranty Trust Company of New York (as Operator of the Euroclear System) published an agreed set of market conventions for the money and bond markets in May 1997 (the "Joint Statement"). They were welcomed by the EMI and the Commission and also by the Bank of England and the BBA, who support their adoption by market participants.

The method of selecting conventions rested on best practice as opposed to choosing the convention used by the largest number of markets. The conventions for the money markets are set out below.

Day Count Basis

5.21   The Joint Statement recommends the use of the actual/360 basis for the wholesale money markets. This, in fact, reflects the practice in most domestic markets in the E.U. and also the practice of the floating rate note market. New loan agreements will adopt this convention. It is expected that advances under legacy agreements will do so too (either because the parties agree it or because

---

[16] See paragraphs 5.40 to 5.60 below.

the agreement allows it). However, there are some loans under which the 365 day convention may have to be followed. To facilitate this, representatives of major banks in the London market are requesting price sponsors to provide rates for in-currencies currently quoted on a 365 day basis on both an actual/360 day and an actual 365/day basis.

Settlement Basis
The Joint Statement recommends the spot/two day standard, which is the prevalent practice for most E.U. currencies.

5.22

Business Days
The Joint Statement recommends that TARGET operating days form the basis for euro business days. TARGET stands for Trans European Automated Real Time Gross Settlement Express Transfer system. This is the system which the E.U. is creating to handle euro wholesale payments. TARGET will operate every day of the year except Saturdays, Sundays, Christmas Day and New Year's Day, provided that the RTGS (standing for the national real time gross settlement) systems of at least two Member States are open. In practice this does not result in any other closed days. The RTGS systems are operated or supervised by the national central banks.

5.23

The major European and London banks will make markets in euro on those days and BBA euro LIBOR and EURIBOR will be quoted on those days for a trade date two TARGET days later.

CHAPS euro will be open on all TARGET operating days and other competing payment mechanisms, such as the Euro Banking Association's euro clearing system, it will also operate on all TARGET operating days.

The days on which the TARGET inter-linking is open will, therefore, be the basis for euro business days for spot values, maturities and rollover dates. New loan agreements should therefore adopt a definition of business day for the purposes of rate setting based on TARGET days, so as to avoid mismatches between rates used in the agreement and rates at which the lender funds itself in the market. Parties to contracts are free to use national business day conventions for payments in euro (and any other purposes), and will probably continue to do so in the case of purely domestic transactions, as full payment services are unlikely to exist on TARGET operating days which are local holidays.[17]

The market associations recommend that these conventions be adopted as standard market practice for financial contracts and instruments entered into or

---

[17] Parties to existing contracts should consider whether the current definition of "business day" will work upon the advent of the euro for payments in euro, particularly as many such definitions refer to days on which banks in the principal financial centre of the relevant currency are "open for business". Although most major banks will be open to make euro payments on days which are TARGET business days, whether they are "open for business" for the purposes of such definition on national holidays in such financial centres is arguable, and will depend upon exactly what business such banks will be conducting on such days and the precise language of the agreement. Banks in London will not at the outset be open for business on bank holidays. Parties will wish to consider the impact of this on their documents, particularly in relation to any rate setting mismatches. Going forward, parties to a contract should ensure their business day definitions cater for these issues.

issued after the Transitional Period begins and for deals entered into beforehand which are intended to redenominate into euro. They recommend that existing conventions should be retained for existing contracts and instruments because of the legal obstacles involved in revising existing contracts and also the dangers of creating hedging mis-matches. In the London market, a group of representatives of major banks, supported by the British Bankers' Association, has suggested that agent banks contact their customers by mid-November 1998 to agree a course of action in relation to those areas in legacy documents which might cause difficulty. Parties may wish to give themselves flexibility going forward by including language providing for the borrower to consult with the bank or agent bank to agree appropriate changes to market conventions at a date in the future; this type of provision is of most value in a syndicated loan where it gives scope for agreeing changes without reference to the syndicate banks.

Increased Costs and Liquid Assets requirements

5.24   It is not yet clear the extent of any costs which the European Central Bank or the European System of Central Banks will impose on banks and whether these will be passed on to borrowers. Reserve requirements (similar to those in relation to minimum liquid assets imposed by the Bank of England in the case of Sterling for some time) are to be imposed by the ECB but the deposits will be remunerated. Banks will need to look at the terms of their legacy documents, in particular at the increased costs clauses, to ensure that they cover not only costs imposed as a result of changes in law or monetary policy by national banks but also any further costs by any central bank or monetary authority with power to impose costs on such bank. Wording commonly adopted in the London market for increased cost clauses will often be sufficiently broad to cover such costs. New agreements may also deal with the issue through a mandatory costs type of formula.

Debt Securities

Continuity of contract

5.25   The issue of continuity of contracts discussed in relation to loan agreements applies equally to debt securities, be it short term paper, notes or bonds, whether privately or publicly issued. Such debt securities may be issued with a fixed rate of interest or floating rate of interest. However, the majority of long-term bonds are fixed rate instruments. The issues raised in relation to fixed rate loan agreements are of added significance here,[18] as an issuer may have issued 20 years ago an instrument with a fixed rate in a market which was not anticipating the possibility of EMU; however, issuers in the long-term capital markets are generally sophisticated entities which know that they are risking the borrowing becoming more expensive if interest rates fall during the lifetime

---

[18] See paragraph 5.12 above.

of their bonds. In practice such entities accept the risk of possibly quite dramatic differences regardless of the circumstances in which they might arise. It is worth noting that documentation does not, as a general rule, allow an issuer to redeem in the event of such changes in the economic environment (unless he can rely on a general right to redeem at his discretion and at a price). Such force majeure clauses are only of relevance in a public issue between signing and closing of the issue and are for the protection of the financial institution lead-managing the issue of the bonds.

Bonds denominated in participating currencies or in Sterling (and other "out" currencies)

The mechanisms for converting payment obligations in participating currencies described in the context of loan agreements in paragraphs 5.03 and 5.05 above apply equally to debt securities.

5.26

Bonds denominated in ECU

The principles described in relation to loan agreements denominated in ECU apply equally where a bond instrument is so denominated. An additional question of interpretation may arise in the bond markets which does not occur in loan agreements. A number of ECU issues provide for a fallback if the ECU is abolished before the maturity of the instrument; it may provide for the instrument to be denominated in one of the currencies included in the ECU basket, or alternatively in a currency, such as US Dollars, which is not a constituent of the ECU basket. There may also be a provision for the instrument to be redeemed upon the disappearance of the ECU.

5.27

These clauses would need to be carefully analysed. Article 2.1 of the First Regulation requires a substitution of the euro for the ECU at the rate of one euro to one ECU. This does not, it is believed, mean that a straightforward substitution of one word for the other is appropriate in all circumstances. In the situation described above where there is a fallback to one of the component currencies of the ECU, it would be meaningless merely to replace the word ECU by the word euro in the sentence which provides for the fallback mechanism as the euro does not have constituent currencies; a court would probably take the view that Article 2.1 deals with the substantive obligation to make payments in ECU and not with a provision which deals with the use of the ECU in the context of another obligation.

As far as the fallback mechanism itself is concerned, the concept of continuity is clearly established in Article 3 of the First Regulation, although it is subject to contrary agreement between the parties to a contract. Therefore a court is likely to feel it appropriate to uphold such a clause in only very limited circumstances and, in most cases, it would probably take the view that the fallback was only intended to apply in the event of a disappearance of the ECU which meant that the contract was incapable of being performed.

Parties to ECU denominated obligations are therefore advised to consider closely the terms of their obligations and to take advice on the matter.

The other issues raised in relation to the ECU in the context of loan contracts arise equally in the debt securities market.

Redenomination

5.28   The question of redenomination is peculiar to the public debt securities market and arises out of the negotiable aspect of public debt issues; it is only relevant in relation to obligations in a participating currency. The term "redenomination" is used to refer to the following processes:

(a) **Simple currency conversion:** this involves restating amounts of interest and principal as amounts in euro at the conversion rate. Payments of interest and principal are made in euro from the date of redenomination. In the absence of such currency conversion, amounts would fall to be payable in the original national currency unit subject to the provisions of Article 8(3) of the Second Regulation.

(b) **Renominalisation:** this involves changing the nominal amount in which the debt securities are held and traded; renominalisation may follow currency conversion if it is felt that it would facilitate trading. Rounding up such nominal amount increases the total amount of the debt; there is no compensatory gain for the issuer and it will need to ensure it does not cause a breach on any limits on borrowing. If it rounds down, an investor suffers a loss for which it will need to be compensated, usually by way of a cash payment. Cashing out will have tax and accounting consequences and may cause hedging mis-matches and is, therefore, to be avoided if at all possible.

(c) **Reconventioning:** this involves changing the terms of outstanding bonds to reflect different market conventions applying to the euro following a redenomination into euro.

This issue of redenomination is separate from that of the quotation, trading and settlement of bonds in the secondary market, which will be conducted in euro in the initially participating countries.

5.29   Private issuers are entitled to redenominate their debt in the national currency unit if the government of that currency has redenominated its public debt. All of the participating Member States will redenominate their public government debt over the conversion weekend but the method by which they will do so will vary. As far as private issues are concerned, market participants have argued strongly against redenominating outstanding issues. The International Primary Markets Association ("IPMA") has not issued any recommendation on the advisability of this. The argument against redenomination is that bonds may be traded in euro whether or not they are redenominated and it would be costly and in some cases cumbersome to do so.

The current understanding is that, despite market recommendation to the contrary, German and Spanish corporate issuers may redenominate over the conversion weekend. The preferred course for non-government issues is to redenominate them at a later date during the Transitional Period either on a limited number of days (preferably a weekend set aside in advance) or on an interest payment date.[19]

---

[19] See Bank of England issue number 8 Practical Issues arising from the Introduction of the Euro page 55, which contains a table setting out market participants, current understanding of the provision in non-government domestic bond markets and participating Member States.

IPMA has enquired as to private issuers' plans, if any, for redenomination and, as of Spring 1998, was currently not aware of any U.K., U.S. or Canadian issuer planning to redenominate bonds issued in "in" currencies.[20]

5.30

Methods by which private issuers can redenominate their bonds vary from jurisdiction to jurisdiction. No governments are planning to make redenomination of the debt of private issuers obligatory but some of them are addressing the need for legislation for redenomination of such debt. Some of these jurisdictions will provide for issuers to redenominate, renominalise and reconvention without reference to bondholders.

However, the redenomination of bonds governed by New York or English law will require bondholders' consent unless specific provision is otherwise made in the terms and conditions of the bonds. Eurobonds governed by English law usually provide for the Trustee (if there is one) to agree to any change to the terms and conditions of the bonds which is of a formal, minor or technical nature or a change which is not materially prejudicial to the bondholders' interests. It might be possible to convince the Trustee that a simple currency conversion would not prejudice the bondholders, and even that a renominalisation with a balancing payment in the event of a rounding down does not prejudice bondholders. Nevertheless, the fact remains that the majority of bond issues specifically provide that a change to the currency of the bond is a matter which requires a special resolution, and sometimes even a higher quorum for such resolution, of bondholders. Although the change from the national currency to the euro arises by operation of law, it is arguable that the conversion of the national currency unit into the euro unit before the end of the Transitional Period, which would occur upon redenomination, is a change in currency which requires bondholders' approval.

IPMA has circulated draft standard form language which is to be used by issuers and investors in new issues (either in currencies participating in EMU or in those which might not do so) where bondholders' consent would otherwise be required. The language covers redenomination, renominalisation and reconventioning.[21] The language provides in summary that:

5.31

(a) the issuer has a discretion whether or not to redenominate and does not require the holders' consent to do so;

(b) the issuer must give 30 days' notice to investors, trustees and paying agents of its wish to redenominate;

(c) redenomination must occur on a coupon date;

(d) the trustee or fiscal agent will be involved in this process;

(e) payments will be in euro units and can no longer be made in national currency units;

---

[20] A peculiar situation arises in relation to bonds denominated in deutschemark, as German legislation provides that these can be redenominated without reference to the governing law of the securities; if that governing law in fact provides that bondholders' consent is required for the redenomination, there is a conflict between the two which an issuer would do best to avoid testing.

[21] See latest draft standard language set out in Appendix 4.

(f) interest is calculated by reference to the aggregate amount of the instruments presented for payment and such payment is rounded to the nearest euro cent.

At the end of the Transitional Period, securities which have not been specifically redenominated will be automatically redenominated (in the narrow sense of converted into euro).

Paying Agents

5.32   It is believed that most paying agents will accept payments in euro or in the national currencies in which the bonds are denominated and convert, generally free of charge, into the other currency.

The International Paying Agents Association released recommendations on June 12, 1998 to issuers of international capital market debt in an effort to ensure a consistent approach to the market in relation to redenomination of legacy bonds and new debt. They stressed that none of the recommendations are intended to conflict with the principle of "no compulsion, no prohibition" and are merely practical suggestions for the market. Their press release is included as Appendix 5.

The international clearing agencies such as Euroclear and Cedel and major national clearing agencies will accept clearing in euro; Cedel and Euroclear will also continue to accept payments in national currencies and allow participants to retain national currency in their multi-currency account.

Market Conventions

5.33   The Joint Statement referred to in paragraph 5.20 above sets out the following conventions for the eurobond markets.

Day Count Basis
5.34   The Joint Statement recommends the use of the actual/actual basis for the eurobond markets, instead of the 30/360 methodology currently used in many E.U. markets, as it is a more exact basis.

Quotation Basis
5.35   The use of decimals rather than fractions is recommended for bond quotations.

Business Days
5.36   The Joint Statement recommends the use of TARGET operating days as the basis for euro business days.

Coupon Frequency
5.37   The choice is between annual and semi-annual payments; no standard practice is recommended in this area as there are strong arguments for both; semi-annual coupons reduce the credit exposure of investors to issuers and are also attractive to institutional investors seeking regular income. It is also the standard most widely used globally. On the other hand annual coupons are used by most E.U. countries, involve lower administrative costs and are attractive to some investors.

Settlement Date

The recommended standard settlement date cycle remains the trade date plus three business days.

5.38

Convertible Bonds

The conversion of share capital into euro may take place either pursuant to the "top down" method, which involves the conversion of the amount of authorised or issued share capital into euro at the appropriate conversion rate and a division by the relevant number of shares or the "bottom up" method, which involves the conversion of the nominal value of each class of share into euro at the appropriate conversion rate, and a multiplication by the relevant number of shares. This may result in the authorised share capital being increased or reduced. Under English law there is no clear method for redenominating share capital.[22]

5.39

The consequences of redenomination of share capital in the context of convertible bonds needs to be examined. The exchange ratio may need to be adjusted; it may be expressed as a number of shares per bond or a number of bonds per share (different methods are used in different jurisdictions and also in different markets). Clearly if the bonds as well as the shares are being redenominated the implications of this would need to be considered.

Derivatives

The areas which have been examined above in relation to loan agreements and bond instruments apply equally, and perhaps more acutely, in relation to derivatives, including foreign exchange contracts.

5.40

Continuity of Contract

It is perhaps in the context of derivatives that the most sensitive questions arise in relation to continuity of contract. The Financial Law Panel[23] identified that the following issues would arise in common commercial situations:

5.41

1. The disappearance of reference indices, particularly in interest rate transactions. The most common example is the basis swap where the parties agree to exchange payments calculated by reference to interest rates on different bases. One party might agree to pay French Franc LIBOR while the other party agrees to pay the FIBOR rate for French Francs. The question is whether the parties can argue that the substitution of EURIBOR for the FIBOR rate and Euro LIBOR for the LIBOR rate achieves a substantially different result from that which was originally contemplated. If that could indeed be shown to be the case it would be difficult for a court to imply that a successor rate should be substituted for the original basis.

---

[22] See Chapter 5 on share capital.
[23] See Financial Law Panel — Economic and Monetary Union — Continuity of Contracts in English Law — January 1998.

2. In derivative contracts the obligation to pay a particular currency may be the commercial purpose of the transaction rather than the method of performing it. This is particularly the case in forward foreign exchange transactions or currency swap transactions. The introduction of the euro effectively transforms the contract into an annuity.

3. Finally, transactions which include an obligation to pay ECU or where the ECU is used as a measure of value may see their nature substantially changed upon the introduction of the euro.

The effect of the First Regulation is that the introduction of the euro will not affect the continuity of these contracts. However, it is anticipated that disputes, if they are to arise, are most likely to do so in the context of derivative transactions and the further work carried out by the banking community and in particular the derivatives market will prove to be fundamental in limiting the scope for such disputes.

Impact of EMU on price sources

5.42   The issues raised by the disappearance of price sources are described in the context of loan agreements.[24] Various industry groupings have identified the need for greater contractual clarity in the context of derivatives and the EMU Protocol[25] seeks to address this and other issues in relation to legacy contracts.

EMU Protocols

5.43   Each institution in the market is expected to conduct the due diligence required to ascertain what EMU issues arise from its business and contracts and to prepare an appropriate plan of action to deal with these issues. In view of some of the particular uncertainties arising out of derivatives contracts and the consequent need to amend current standardised documents to eliminate any legal uncertainty, ISDA, and more recently the British Bankers' Association, in conjunction with the New York Financial Markets Lawyers Group, have devised certain provisions to facilitate the process in the context of ISDA and IFEMA/FEOMA/ICOM Master Agreements.

ISDA EMU Protocol
5.44   The first step for ISDA was to publish in July 1997 continuity language to clarify that parties are not able to walk away unilaterally from their contract as a result of the introduction of the euro. ISDA then published an updated standard definition of the ECU, taking account of the First Regulation. It has also been developing language to deal with changes to current national rate sources, payment netting, business and banking day definitions and the definition of ECU Settlement Day.

In view of the large number of standard changes which would be necessary to clarify the position in relation to existing ISDA Master Agreements, ISDA

---

[24] See paragraphs 5.15 to 5.19 above.
[25] See paragraphs 5.43 to 5.52 below.

considered how such changes could be implemented in the most practical and efficient manner. Clearly individual negotiations between counterparties would be time consuming and expensive. It has therefore devised a practical solution in the form of the EMU Protocol.[26] This is a multilateral protocol enabling individual institutions to agree amendments to their outstanding contracts. Parties are able to select from a list of five provisions those which they wish to adopt and, once a party has signed an "Adherence Letter", it has effectively made an offer to one or more counterparties to amend any outstanding agreements between them to the extent that the other adhering parties make matching elections.

5.45

The Protocol can be used by any bank, corporation, government, pension fund and other legal entity (it is not intended to be used by individuals in the same way as the Master Agreement itself is not so intended). Such party need not be a member of ISDA to adhere. Interested parties can visit ISDA's website and obtain the Protocol from there. Attached to the Protocol is an Adherence Letter the signed original of which, together with a conformed copy, is required to be sent to ISDA's offices in London or New York. Names for adhering parties are listed on ISDA's website where there is access to scanned copies of Adherence Letters.

Once an Adherence Letter has been accepted by ISDA that firm is bound by all amendments in respect of parties who adhered to the Protocol and made matching elections. The Protocol is designed to leave credit support arrangements unaffected.

If the parties wish to check the signing authority of Protocol adherents they will need to do so directly; the Adherence Letter includes the name and contact details for each adhering institution for that purpose.

The Protocol was open for adherence between May 6, and September 30, 1998; adherence ended at the end of September to allow time for system changes and also for parties to negotiate and agree changes with counterparties who have not adhered to the Protocol.

Parties were able to specify a cut-off date in respect of their own adherence as a result of which the adherence of any of their counterparties after that date would have been ineffective in respect of an ISDA Master Agreement between them.

The Protocol is intended to cover ISDA Master Agreements regardless of the governing law of the agreement.

It does not address all EMU considerations that might exist in relation to a derivative transaction and parties are advised to consider any other issues that arise out of their documents (for instance, equity based derivatives give rise to certain issues described below and may require separate amendment). The Protocol itself cannot be amended and any additional changes need to be dealt with separately on a bilateral basis.

The Protocol seeks to address issues in existing contractual arrangements. Parties will wish to deal with these issues in contracts going forward either by specific reference or possibly by a more general incorporation of the terms of the Protocol. They will also be able to incorporate into their confirmations the most up-to-date set of 1998 ISDA Euro Definitions.

---

[26] See Appendix 2.

The areas which it addresses are the following:

(a) confirmation of continuity of contract;

(b) confirmation of applicable successor price sources;

(c) clarification of payment netting between participating currencies;

(d) new and amended definitions for euro, ECU, ECU Settlement Day, Business Day and Banking Day;

(e) provision for adjustment of bond options in the event of redenomination of the underlying bonds.

Confirmation of continuity of contract

5.46   The continuity provision clarifies the position for jurisdictions where there is no continuity legislation and merely confirms the provisions for those jurisdictions which have passed continuity legislation (namely the E.U. and certain U.S. States).

Price sources election

5.47   The intention of the provision is to avoid confusion over the switch to successor rates and further reliance on reference banks as a fallback. It confirms that contracts continue to function in the case of changing price sources by:

(a) using the new rate appearing on the existing screen page in place of the old rate;

(b) if there is no rate on the existing screen page, using the officially designated successor rate;

(c) if no successor rate is officially designated, using the EURIBOR screen page;

(d) if the EURIBOR screen page is not available, using reference banks.

The provision also clarifies that existing day count conventions and fixing periods continue to apply, even if EURIBOR is the appropriate successor (EURIBOR may be based on different day count fractions or fixing periods from the original interbank offered rate).

Payment netting

5.48   The existing language of Section 2(c) of the ISDA Master Agreement would require netting of payments in participating currency units which were different currencies prior to the introduction of the euro. Where the parties had originally provided for netting to occur in relation to payments in the same currency but not for cross currency netting, they may wish to override payment netting in this limited case, in the event that their back office is not able to undertake such payment netting.

Changes to definitions

5.49   The Protocol provides for a definition of the euro and makes changes to the definitions of ECU, ECU Settlement Day, Business Day and Banking Day.

The definition of Business Day in particular is of interest; recitals to the changes make clear that the intention is threefold:

(a) to recognise that payments in euro may be settled by commercial banks and in foreign exchange markets in a place and on a day on which commercial banks in that place would otherwise be closed for business;

(b) to recognise that from the beginning of the Transitional Period all payments expressly payable in the national currency unit would technically be payable in euro and that there may be no readily identifiable principal financial centre for the euro;

(c) to preserve the existing position where a payment obligation is payable in or calculated by reference to a national currency unit by agreeing that days on which commercial banks and foreign exchange markets are open in a place solely for the purpose of settling payments in the euro should not be considered days in which payments in a national currency unit can be settled in that place and that references to the principal financial centre of a national currency unit shall continue to bear the same meaning throughout the term of the transaction.

Bond options
In the event that an underlying bond is redenominated (renominalised or reconventioned as well as converted) into euro, the value of the bond option may be affected and changes may be required to strike prices or payments. The Protocol provides for a standard amendment whereby the calculation agent makes the necessary adjustments.   **5.50**

Financial Markets Lawyers Group/British Bankers' Association EMU Protocol
This Protocol, just recently published, is modelled after and includes language from the ISDA Protocol.[27] Its adherence procedure is similar; adherence letters must be received by no later than November 30, 1998. It does, however, differ in some material respects from the ISDA Protocol. The areas it covers are: **5.51**

(a) confirmation of continuity;

(b) provision of replacement price sources;

(c) clarification of payment netting and novation netting;

(d) new definitions relating to the euro;

(e) provisions for average rate options;

(f) provisions for barrier options.

Market conventions

The Joint Statement sets out the following conventions for the foreign exchange markets: **5.52**

---

[27] See Appendix 2.

- the settlement basis is the spot/two day standard basis;

- the quotation basis is certain for uncertain (*e.g.* one euro = x foreign currency).

It also sets out the following conventions for swaps:

- the floating side follows the money market convention;

- the fixed side follows the bond market convention (of semi-annual payments). However, as the bond markets could not agree on the need for the payment basis to be semi-annual, agreements may need to vary in this respect to ensure that no mis-match occurs in regard to any underlying bond. ISDA is currently consulting its members on this point.

Expected market practice in the derivatives market

5.53   ISDA has set up an operations task force to provide guidance to derivatives back office operations on the implications of EMU. Some of their recommendations, although not of a legal nature as such, are interesting in understanding the general impact that the introduction of the euro will have on derivatives legal documentation[28] ISDA has considered separately interest rate products and bond, equity and foreign exchange derivatives. An overview of these provisions is set out below:

Interest rate products
5.54   ISDA identified five types of transaction:

(i) Transactions dealt after the start of Stage 3 of EMU ("eurodeals").
   It is expected that all "eurodeals" on the interbank market will be traded in the euro unit. As far as such transactions with corporates are concerned, new transactions are expected increasingly to be denominated in the euro unit although new transactions for small corporates and retail counterparties may continue to be traded in national currency units until much later in the Transitional Period. The new market conventions would apply to all new transactions and the reference rates for euro denominated transactions are expected to be either Euro LIBOR or EURIBOR.

(ii) Outstanding transactions in in-currencies existing at the start of the Transitional Period and maturing before the end of it ("transitional legacy deals").
   Pursuant to the E.U. Regulations there is no intention to force counterparties into a redenomination of their existing portfolio of derivative transactions.[29] All original terms of the contract will probably prevail, certainly at the very beginning of the Transitional Period,

---

[28] See ISDA EMU Guidebook for a fuller account of their recommendations.
[29] This follows the principle of "no compulsion, no prohibition".

subject to certain key terms changing (see discussion on price sources above). If the parties wish to express their contract in euro they are free to do so by mutual agreement. It is thought however that other features such as day count fractions, payment schedules and market conventions should remain the same but payment netting will need to be considered.[30]

(iii) Outstanding transactions in in-currencies maturing after the end of the Transitional Period ("long-term legacy deals").

In light of the Second Regulation which in effect provides an automatic form of redenomination at the end of the Transitional Period, it is expected that market participants will not amend existing agreements to redenominate them as this will happen in any event; therefore, the same approach applies as in the case of transitional legacy deals. The end of the Transitional Period will require changes to settlement arrangements; however, there is no market consensus currently in this area and the ISDA task force feels it is premature to establish one.

(iv) Transactions denominated in ECU at the start of the Transitional Period ("legacy ECU deals").

5.55

In view of the First Regulation which automatically prescribes the replacement of the ECU by the euro, there appears to be no need for market participants to redenominate or convert existing ECU values as this happens automatically. Parties may wish to change their settlement procedures to settle explicitly the euro. With regard to Business Days, the ISDA EMU Protocol provides clarification of the definition of ECU Settlement Day.

(v) Transactions explicitly in euro entered into before the start of the Transitional Period ("forward euro deals").

Participants may wish to enter into transactions specifically referring to the euro prior to the beginning of the Transitional Period. This could be achieved by the parties agreeing to book a transaction in ECU (which will convert to the euro on a one-to-one basis) but applying the new euro conventions. Care needs to be taken in the choice of price sources to ensure that a euro price source would apply. Alternatively, if the deal is structured at the outset in euro, care needs to be taken in respect of accounting implications in particular.

Bond Options and Asset Swaps
ISDA have distinguished between instances where there is no reconventioning and "not significant renominalisation" and instances where there is reconventioning and significant renominalisation:

5.56

(a) no reconventioning and "not-significant renominalisation":

— ISDA believes that existing references to nominal amounts of bonds should be simply read as equivalent euro references

---

[30] See Protocol above.

applying the rounding/renominalisation rule to the underlying instrument. It also does not believe there is a need to make any adjustments to the strike price for the option, given that the economic value of the underlying instrument has not changed. Where cash settlement takes place, the option writer could fulfil his payment obligations by settling either in euro or the legacy national currency unit. In the case of physical settlement the writer of the option would have an obligation to deliver the underlying bonds which are not denominated in euro in accordance with the previously agreed nominal amount. In the case of renominalisation to the euro, there would be no payment of the cash difference as this amount would be immaterial;

— as far as asset swaps and repackagings are concerned, there would be no material mis-match arising between the underlying bond and the associated interest rate swap, and ISDA does not therefore see any need to adjust existing arrangements. However, even very minor rounding differences could create problems with structures involving special purpose vehicles which are intended to be bankruptcy remote and the analysis of the impact of redenomination on such vehicles needs to be carefully considered.

5.57   (b) reconventioning and significant renominalisation:

— in this case the economic value of the underlying bond is changed and the bond option is therefore affected. ISDA believes it is preferable to adjust this by allowing calculation agents to adjust the strike price rather than by adjusting premiums. This is the approach followed in the ISDA EMU Protocol. In this case, renominalisation of greater than one euro will affect the economic value of the instrument and this change needs to be addressed, preferably by retaining the existing strike price and making a cash settlement in respect of the rounded/cashed out amount. ISDA recommends that amounts of less than 100 euro be disregarded and that transactions be reconfirmed at this point and also that the parties include provisions in new transactions to deal with the above approach. Where reconventioning affects the economic value of an instrument in a material way, ISDA has recommended that calculation agents be empowered to adjust strike prices to ensure that values of the option stay the same. Any such adjustments should be reconfirmed at the time that they occur. Other settlement issues are the same as described above. Similar problems arise under options on bond futures;

— with regard to asset swaps and repackaging, reconventioning and significant renominalisation will lead to material mis-match between the underlying bond and the associated swap. Parties must therefore carefully assess the implications on these structures, particularly where special purpose vehicles are concerned.

Equity Derivatives

The distinction here is in relation to shares quoted on in-country exchanges **5.58**
and those quoted on out-country exchanges.

(a) Options on single shares quoted on in-country exchanges: it is anticipated that there will be a switch to euro denominated trading at the
beginning of the Transitional Period.

(b) Options on stock indexes for in-country exchanges: no particular issues
have been identified here, as long as the relevant index is not rebased or
merged with another index to reflect changes made to the european
equities market, plans for which are not however currently
contemplated.

(c) Options on single shares quoted on out-country exchanges: such shares
may also be traded in euro and this will affect the strike price of any
related option. The issue here is that timing of the switch to euro
denomination is less certain and will vary from exchange to exchange
and from share to share and the question then arises as to the
appropriate conversion rate to be applied. ISDA recommends here that
the strike price be adjusted in line with the approach of the relevant
futures market; this should probably occur at the time that trading in the
underlying shares switches to euro.

(d) Options on stock indices for out-country exchanges: further complication arises here in that some of the constituent shares may move to euro
trading while others do not. As this effect will be manifest in the index
and reflected in the futures price, the recommendation by ISDA is to
adjust in line with the approach of the relevant futures market.

Foreign Exchange Derivatives

(a) Existing contracts in ECU: these should be treated in the same manner **5.59**
as interest rate contracts, with references to ECU being read as references to euro.

(b) In/in-currency contracts: where two in-currencies are involved, firms
will probably wish to rationalise their portfolios to remove such transactions, although there should be no presumption to close these out and
any early termination needs to be by mutual agreement. Counterparties
may in fact wish to keep the legacy transaction in place either to offset
separate currency cash flows continuing into the Transitional Period or
for tax considerations.

(c) In/out-currency contracts: here, any legacy in-currencies should simply
be treated as amounts in euro. Parties may wish to amend the existing
transaction to explicitly change over from the legacy national currency
to the euro and they will need also to change payment and settlement
arrangements to achieve this.[31]

---

[31] The ISDA EMU Guidebook sets out certain issues arising in relation to barrier options and
average rate and similar options.

6

The Technology Issues Arising as a Result of Economic and Monetary Union

by Heather Rowe, Lovell White Durrant

Introduction — What is the problem?

Other Chapters of this book will be examining the legal framework adopted by the European Commission for the introduction of the euro and the general legal issues in relation to the introduction of the euro. This Chapter specifically examines the information technology issues that businesses will need to consider or areas where information technology matters may need to be dealt with. It assumes, given that all areas relating to the introduction of the euro are dealt with elsewhere, a level of familiarity with the basic provisions relating to the introduction of the euro.

6.01

Looking at the technology issues arising as a result of the introduction of Economic and Monetary Union (EMU), it must be said that there are not many legal issues to address. The legal issues arise, most obviously, when considering how loan agreements or financial documentation needs to be amended to recognise the advent of EMU. However, a huge part of the cost of the introduction of EMU will be the cost of the necessary changes to technology and, therefore, it is crucial for all those who are looking at matters arising from the introduction of EMU to have some understanding of the technology issues.

Although the U.K. is not going to enter EMU in the first wave, there are still legal and business reasons why every U.K. company needs to at least consider the impact of EMU, to see if it does apply to them:

6.02

— the rules laid out in the First Regulation will still apply to the U.K. (including the rules on conversion and rounding);

— companies with subsidiaries in participating countries, or which themselves are a subsidiary of such a company, will need to consider the implications of this on corporate trading, as well as reporting and central accounting;

— companies need to consider the effect of the euro on their pricing strategies;

— companies need to consider their banking and treasury arrangements after January 1, 1999 and their need to settle or receive payment in euros.

6.03   The Confederation of British Industry stresses that U.K. companies "in the front line" include those that:

(a) export from or import to countries involved in EMU;

(b) have competitors who export from the EMU zone;

(c) are multinationals doing business within the EMU zone;

(d) have ownership or investment links with the EMU zone;

(e) are part of a supply chain which includes a multinational or exporter;

(f) are a bank or financial company involved in foreign business operations;

(g) are involved in the travel or tourism industries.

That is a large number of companies. These are also the ones with the greatest requirements for changes to their I.T. systems to cope with the fact that it is essential they deal with euros, preferably from day one of EMU.

U.K. businesses may think that because the United Kingdom will be outside EMU when it commences, that minimal changes will be required because we will have "business as usual" and the pound in one's pocket will still be the pound in one's pocket. Whilst this is true, for all of the companies described above, if they need to handle euros for the purposes of their business, their software will need to be changed to accommodate this.

Conversion to the euro and rounding

6.04   Even though the U.K. will not join the EMU in the first wave, U.K. companies will still, if it is relevant to them, have to have the ability to account for and deal with the euro as a foreign currency and to calculate currency conversions into euros; which will require an ability to deal with conversion and rounding. All major U.K. companies with dealings with other states participating in the euro and/or with business partners or offices in other Member States must address this problem. This will include banks obviously, financial and legal firms in the City, as well as any export based manufacturers.

Multinational enterprises that use the same information systems for all their operations may have to upgrade information systems located both inside and outside the Euro zone in order to maintain compatibility.

If the U.K. "opts in" in the future the changes required will be more extensive. Even domestic-only software will need to be amended to replace sterling with the euro. At present, software being written in the U.K. primarily assumes that all payments in the U.K. are to be in sterling, so substantial systems modifications will be needed to cope with the advent of the euro.

Conversion between Participating National Currencies

Conversion from one participating national currency unit into another during the Transitional Period is a significant I.T. challenge because it will involve a three step process (known as "triangulation"):

6.05

(i) convert to the euro from the first currency at the fixed conversion rate, with the result rounded to not less than three decimals;

(ii) convert the resulting amount in euro to the second currency at the relevant fixed conversion rate; and

(iii) round the final result to the nearest sub-unit.

It is the result, rather than the method itself, which is important, so other methods of calculation may be used if they produce the same answer. However, this is complex and may require complex solutions and software changes. Current software simply does not work this way to convert Currency A into Currency B — the intermediate step is absent.

Inverse rates and rounding differences

The conversion rate for converting existing currencies to the euro will be based on one euro expressed in terms of each participating national currency to six significant figures (not decimal places). So, using a hypothetical example which has been used by the Bank of England to explain how this will work, one euro might be equal to FF 6.58001 or DM 1.92003. The conversion rate may not be truncated or rounded when making conversions: for instance, it may not be shortened to FF 6.58 in the above example.

6.06

If the result of conversion is not an exact number, it will be rounded up or down to the nearest sub-unit. If this produces a result exactly half-way, the sum will be rounded up.

Inverse conversion rates for converting between a national currency unit and the euro is prohibited by Article 4.3 of the First Regulation because this method can cause rounding differences. The Commission has published an example using GBP as a hypothetical example to show this.

Assume the following conversion rates:

6.07

Conversion rate: EUR 1 = £ 0.704182
Inverse rate (10 digits): EUR 1.420087421 = £1

	GBP	EUR
Conversion rate	7,500,000	10,650,655.65
Inverse rate	7,500,000	10,650,655.66

Despite the high accuracy (10 digits) the inverse rate method still results in a rounding difference. This is only 1p in £7,500,000; but, it illustrates the point that, for large amounts, rounding differences can occur.

6.08   Article 4.3 of the First Regulation is part of English law. This provides that conversions either way between the euro and "national currency units" will be effected at the "conversion rates". It goes on to state that inverse rates derived from the "conversion rates" will not be used. The expression "national currency units" is defined to mean the units of the currencies of participating Member States (as those units exist immediately before the start of the third stage of EMU). The expression "participating Member State" is defined to mean a Member State which adopts the euro in accordance with the Treaty. The expression "conversion rates" is defined to mean the irrevocably fixed conversion rates which the European Council is to adopt in accordance with Article 109.l(4) of the Treaty (this is expected to happen on December 31, 1998).

The rule against the use of inverse rates applies to all E.U. Member States but only when converting between the euro and the national currency unit of a participating Member State. It would apply to a U.K. company when converting between euro units and Deutschemark units after January 1, 1999; but it would not apply to conversions between euro units and sterling units unless and until the U.K. participates. However, as a practical matter, there might be some sense in a system adopting a methodology which is broadly consistent, whether converting between two "in" currencies or between an "in" currency and an "out" currency.

Balancing Errors

6.09   Accounting software has been designed to balance to the nearest cent/penny. In converting accounts from national currency units to the euro balancing errors will occur. Decisions will be required as to how the accounts are to be balanced — whether the higher or the lower amount is taken and the difference written off.

Although the Regulations have been designed to minimise the effect of conversion and rounding errors, it is impossible to eliminate them completely. Rounding errors could arise:

(i) when converting individual items and cumulative amounts based on the same items.

(ii) where amounts are converted back and forth between currencies.

Historical Information

6.10   When enterprises change over to the euro, the historical financial information denominated in the national currency unit will then have to be converted to euro. Though not all historical financial information may be equally relevant, it is necessary to convert all data that has a future use to the euro.

The Commission has stressed that converting historical financial information poses a significant problem for virtually all financial information systems, even those that have a "foreign currency" module that can handle foreign currencies. The following options are available to convert historical data:

(a) **Manual conversion:**

This requires that all historical data is manually translated into euro and then input into the financial information system. This solution has the twin disadvantages that is its very susceptible to errors and is labour intensive. Nevertheless, in the case of financial information systems that keep little historical data it may be the most cost efficient alternative, rather than purchasing new software or rewriting the systems.

(b) **Conversion automatically:**

The historical information can also be converted automatically, but this requires the development of a special one-off conversion utility. Developing such a conversion utility can be fairly easy when the financial information system is based on a relatively "standard" (relational) database management system. However, in the case of proprietary data formats specially created by a company for its own systems, developing a conversion utility may be quite a daunting task. The conversion may require some extra processing time and hence will need an associated review of processing capacity.

6.11

(c) **Modify the existing information system:**

In this case the conversion utility is built into the financial information system and forms part of the added 'euro functionality' of the system. This method probably offers the most flexibility to the user of the financial information system but there will be a cost involved.

(d) **Encapsulation:**

All historic financial information continues to be stored in the original national currency units but all input and output is converted to and from the euro unit. Encapsulation can only be a temporary solution because converting all input and output is burdensome; and the information systems will tend to generate rounding differences.

Decimals

Financial information systems that were designed to work with a national currency unit without decimals will need to be altered in order to work with euro cents. Both the peseta and the lira are currently expressed without decimals.

6.12

Interfaces

Developing interfaces between systems that use different currency units is often more complicated than expected — for example, because of the need to deal with rounding differences.

When different financial information systems change over to the euro at different times, problems can arise with communication between those systems. Several approaches exist to tackle the interface problem:

6.13

(a) **Build converters:**

Building interfaces that not only link two systems, but that also convert the amounts from one currency unit to the other. However, the European Commission has pointed out that technical problems (such as rounding) can make this approach very unattractive;

(b) **Simultaneous changeover:**

6.14   Changing all information systems to the euro at the same time. This eliminates the need for interfaces between information systems that convert amounts to and from euro;

(c) **Autonomous groups:**

Identifying groups of information systems that are relatively autonomous, having little or no links to other information systems. These groups of information systems could be changed over to the euro at different times, while requiring fewer interfaces that can convert between currency units. This approach, which combines some of the advantages and disadvantages of (a) and (b) above, can be a practical solution in some situations.

Displaying two currencies

6.15   Displaying information in two currency units at the same time can be difficult because the amount of space (number of columns) available on computer displays and printed reports is limited.

Keyboards and use of the euro symbol

6.16   I.T. systems generate output which will be printed on either blank stationery or on pre-printed stationery, such as invoices, statements, etc. with a euro symbol instead of the £ sign.

The International Standards Organisation ISO4217 Maintenance Agency adopted the currency code "EUR" for the euro on April 21, 1997 with immediate effect. Now the "EUR" has been chosen, the effect on print layouts for blank and pre-printed stationery will be wide ranging. In fact, many forms do not show a currency symbol. Therefore, to avoid confusion during the transition, a currency symbol may need to be introduced. This may cause the need for considerable form redesign and reprogramming because of the possibly different number of characters involved.

The euro will be worth less than a pound and thus numerical euro amounts will be larger, possibly exceeding existing field sizes.

The symbol for the euro was originally unveiled at the Dublin Summit. The Commission has published a Communication setting out the technical specification for the euro symbol and announcing its own intention to use it — inviting others to do the same. It is not obligatory to do so.

6.17   The symbol has not been greeted with universal warmth — indeed, many technology companies make the point that if the euro is going to be represented by the letters "EUR", then a symbol should not be made obligatory.

Computer users can simply type "EUR" and no special keyboard key needs to be created for this. Were the symbol to be made obligatory, it would require all keyboards to be changed (at considerable expense) and computer programming languages would have to be changed to be able to create this new symbol. Other types of input devices might also need alteration (or replacement). The I.T. industry, in many sectors, questions the cost/benefit analysis of widespread use of the symbol and the changes it would necessitate.

Continental countries use a full stop as a thousands separator and a comma as a decimal point, which is the reverse of the British convention. Whether the euro will be subject to either or both of these conventions is not yet clear. However continental counterparts may be confused by the British convention and vice-versa. So companies will need to make it clear which convention they are using.

All the above considerations apply not only to printed reports and forms, but also to screen layouts and keyboard mapping.

The Technology Context

The software industry and most companies are (just about) getting to grips **6.18** with the prospect of the "Millennium Meltdown" (and how to deal with it).

The Millennium problem arises because the majority of computer systems use two digit data fields to recognise dates, instead of four. For example, the year 1996 is recognised as 96. In some cases programs will take January 1, 2000, when it arrives, annotate it as 01/01/00, or as being the year 1900, or will not recognise that date, possibly even causing the computer to crash. Alternatively, data could be corrupted and dates not registered.

Hot on the heels of the Millennium problem is a problem which, in actual fact, may need to be addressed before the Millennium problem by some companies — namely the steps needed to deal with EMU — and by the year 1999, not 2000 — if they want to compete with banks and other companies within the "euro zone".

One could say that the Year 2000 problem is essentially a technical one, **6.19** whereas EMU poses much more fundamental problems requiring potential functional changes to systems. In most cases the Millennium problem is the one that needs to be sorted out first (or, at least, the assessment of the size of the problem, on the basis that there are far more software programmes and computer chips dependent on dates and far more realistic prospects of complete system crashes than there will be from changes to accommodate the euro). Nevertheless, steps to create euro-compliant systems must follow very shortly behind Millennium changes or in parallel. Companies should already be planning for the changes which might be required. Indeed, some U.K. programmes may need to change by January 1, 1999 if they are to be used to calculate conversion and rounding.

The London Investment Banking Association has said "for many systems, assume an 18 month period for developing and testing". In that case, for many it is already too late to be ready by January 1, 1999.

The Cost

The Financial Sector

6.20   Barclays Bank have indicated publicly that they could spend in excess of £250,000,000 in the process. This is more than its estimated spend on the Millennium problem.

The Association for Payment Clearing Services (APACS) has estimated that the cost to banks will be at least £914,000,000 at 1994 prices, including a spend of £436,000,000 on systems over three years. In actual fact, APACS, which runs most of the U.K.'s inter-bank settlement and cheque clearing services, have now said that that estimate (given back in 1995) can probably be doubled.

The Retail Sector

6.21   On the assumption that the U.K. joined EMU, The British Retail Consortium reckoned that plans for the euro would cost around £1.7 billion (up from £1.5 billion about a year ago) — just to change point of sale systems. They have been looking at their estimates of costs of introducing EMU and they have expressed a view that EMU would cost up to three per cent of retailers' turnover. Indeed, they suggested a total figure for U.K. retailers of £3.5 billion if the U.K. joined EMU in the first wave.

In May of 1996, Marks & Spencer (M&S) suggested to a House of Commons Committee that, at worst, EMU would cost them £100,000,000. They would need to replace tills; buy other hardware; replace or amend existing software; and provide a lot of training. Subsequently M&S said the cost will be between £10,000,000 and £50,000,000 rather than the higher figure, because they would phase in conversion gradually. Because some of the changes would not be required until after the Year 2000, the rolling project approach should give sufficient time to introduce all the changes necessary.

In 1998 M&S (and Tesco) were reported in the *Financial Times* as quoting around £30million each. There would be additional costs for M&S of a "big bang" conversion of coin handling facilities in their overseas stores in participating member states when euro coins and notes arrive in 2002.

Some European Banking Statistics

6.22   A study in 1997 by the European Banking Federation estimated the overall cost of conversion as being ECU 8-10 billion, representing two per cent of annual operating costs over three years of the transition. Significant budgets are being allocated for staff training and customer education. That echoes a British Bankers' Association estimate for the cost to the average bank of a "big-bang" style conversion to a single currency as being two per cent of annual expenses. Spreading the work over two or three years of a phased introduction will be less problematic than a sudden big-bang changeover, but possibly more expensive.

Generale Bank has estimated it would spend two billion Belgian Francs ($65 million) on the project; Deutsche Bank estimates DM 300 million; and Dresdner

Bank estimates that Germany's smaller banks, just to allow data processing in the single currency, will need to invest DM 2 million for each DM 1 billion of balance sheet assets. Groupe Paribas has allocated FF 300m (£35 million).

The Gartner Group, a major computer consultancy, estimates that the Europe-wide software conversion costs for the euro will be $100 billion.

Who Will do the Work and When?

A major problem is that, given all the work that is already taking place in relation to Year 2000, software developers and specialist consultants are going to be heavily stretched to be able to make, for example, euro-compliant inter-bank settlement systems by January 1, 1999. Salaries for I.T. personnel and fees for consultants are rising rapidly, to keep abreast of demand, much of it engendered by the need to address Year 2000 issues.

6.23

Jackie Olivier, a Director of Trans Millennium Services at Cap Gemini U.K. (formerly Hoskyns), providers of software development and consultancy, has said "the paradox of the EMU versus Millennium debate is that both problems have the capability to destroy your organisation. If you don't fix the Year 2000 problem you won't be in business after January 1, 2000. But if you don't decide how to handle the challenge of EMU, you won't be in business for all that much longer".

The Business and Accounting Software Developers' Association ("BASDA") estimated, in November 1997 that, for a medium sized company with a single site installation, conversion will take approximately 9-12 months. For a multi-site large company the estimate is 18-24 months, and for large banks and very large corporations the estimate is 36-48 months. However, these are simply estimates. The timetable for I.T. conversion to the euro will vary considerably from company to company.

Companies need to allow sufficient time not only for assessing and changing their software but also for testing of systems, both for correct application performance and for compliance, which will be a major component of the transition project and may take up more than 50 per cent of the time allocated for the project.

In systems terms, the real problems are going to arise in four areas:

(a) older or "legacy" systems;

(b) complex systems;

(c) systems which have been heavily customised or had extra modules "bolted on" over the years;

(d) the data structure.

Older Systems

In the case of older systems, there is a very real danger that the user could almost be held to ransom by the software industry as there will be very few programmers still around with the necessary know how. It is rumoured that

6.24

the relatively few programmers who are familiar with some of the older programming languages like COBOL can command premium salaries. Think of the premium they will command by the Millennium — and they will still be required to help deal with problems after that date. It is a fact that not all software can possibly be made EMU or Millennium compliant in the time that is left.

Complex Systems

6.25   The more complicated the system, the longer the time required to analyse the changes that might be necessary to accommodate the introduction of the euro. The more complex the system, the more likely that, as in the case of older systems, there is a shortage of programmers to deal with the necessary reprogramming. Alternatively, the changes might simply be too numerous to effect in the time frame.

Heavily Modified Systems

6.26   In the case of heavily modified systems, similar concerns will arise. There may only be one software house or a handful of people capable of carrying out the work — and they will no doubt already be fully occupied. Indeed, EMU will bring strategic opportunities for software houses, as the one which produces new user friendly "EMU — compliant" systems stands to do very well. It may well be the only answer for some companies to replace problematic software; even at a cost, rather than modify it.

If the changes were made in-house, the relevant employees with the necessary skills may have left. Perhaps worse, the programmers' notes or functional specifications relating to changes made over the years may be lost, incomplete or non-existent. Many such programmes are still in use, heavily amended over the years and, without the necessary details of the changes, further changes will be very difficult.

The Data Structure

6.27   The way data is structured may complicate issues. Questions need to be asked as to whether all data should be converted at the same time, or converted gradually, and what data should be copied.

Also, master data held on a computer may need changing for EMU compliance. For example, a low value item such as a nut or bolt costing a few French centimes, could easily be translated by the system as zero euros if rounded to just a few numbers. Hence changes might be needed to the master data detailing units of measure, for instance, so that systems always calculate the quantity of bolts in thousands, as opposed to single units so as to give the unit a value.

Legal Issues in Changing Software

Before discussing the legal issuing it is necessary to understand in very general terms how programming is carried out. A computer programmer will write a software program in a high level language such as COBOL and that master version of the code is called the "source code"; sometimes called human readable code or something similar. This is written in some form of algorithm, for example, or may look a bit like a flow chart. Whilst not comprehensible to most, a computer programmer reading the source code will understand how the software is being constructed and, much more importantly, how it might be changed. This master code is essential. Without it, one cannot change the content of software.

6.28

If the source code of a program was fed into a computer, it would not understand it. Computers work in binary. They recognise only zero or one: off or on, electric pulse off or electric pulse on. The next step, therefore, is to convert the source code into binary language, so that a computer will understand it.

This involves running the source code through a "compiler" which converts the source code into a binary form. This binary form is call "object code" or "machine code" because it is then in a form understood by a computer. However, once compiled, to make a change to the copy in object code, it will be necessary to have the source code, to make the appropriate change to the source code, and then to recompile that source code to generate an amended object code version.

Before embarking on changes to give effect to the advent of EMU, a company will need to satisfy itself that it has the legal right to make those changes; which means a legal right to use the source code for this purpose.

If the software has been written especially for a company, often called "bespoke software", the ownership of the intellectual property rights (effectively, copyright) in the source code will quite often belong to the company using it. This will be the case under English copyright law if the code has been written by an employee of that company in the ordinary course of that employee's employment, since Section 11(2) of the Copyright, Designs and Patents Act 1988 provides for employee works, broadly speaking, to belong to their employer.

6.29

The more tricky situation is where a company has (as it often does) employed a consultant to write the software. Where the author is not an employee of the company, copyright will belong to the author (Section 11(1) of the Copyright Designs and Patents Act 1988). If the author is a consultant, and there is nothing in the software development contract vesting title to the intellectual property rights in the customer, then the copyright in that program will belong to the consultant. There should always therefore be an express clause passing all rights in the software to the client company.

If there is no such clause, this may not prove an absolute bar to the company using that software because it is quite likely that, as between the commissioner of the software who has paid for it and the consultant, there will be an implied licence for the company to use the software. Where matters can get a little more complicated, in such circumstances, is where the customer does not have the ability, itself, to make the changes but would like to employ a third party to do this. A "canny" consultant, who has written a program for a customer, and does not relish the idea of a competitor having access to its valuable source code, may try to prevent disclosure by the customer of that program to a third party. It could well succeed in this since it owns the software and any implied licence for the software would be personal to the user. Indeed, in many agreements there might be confidentiality provisions which might prevent such a disclosure.

6.30   It is therefore crucial, if one is concerned about this issue, to check the terms of appointment of consultants writing software. This could include, if there is a concern whether a consultant has power to pass title to software (assuming there is a clause in the contract passing title to the copyright in the software), checking that its employees wrote the program, thereby vesting it in the consultant so that the consultant can then pass title to its client. Indeed, it may even be worthwhile checking that a user's own employees involved in the writing of the software did so in the ordinary course of their employment.

If title to the software does not pass to the user, the user should insist on an express licence to use the software, preferably including use of the source code for maintenance purposes, with ability to disclose the source code (on a confidential basis) to third party software maintainers.

It should also be borne in mind that most software particularly off the shelf, standard software will not be owned to the companies using it, but only licensed to them — and then probably in "object code" only. This means that those companies will almost certainly be unable to amend the software, either because the terms of their licence prohibit it and/or because they cannot do so without the source code. Software houses very rarely allow access to the source code to licensees if they can avoid it; because this effectively ties licensees to them for future maintenance and enhancement, as licensees cannot amend the software without the source code.

6.31   It may be possible to "reverse engineer" the binary version of a software program back to the source code but it is expensive to do and requires a lot of computing power. Many software licences forbid reverse engineering, in any event.

Many companies have the source code of their software deposited "in escrow" by the software supplier with a trusted third party like The National Computing Centre (NCC), but it is unlikely the escrow deposit would be triggered. Escrow arrangements are really designed to protect licensees and allow them to access the copy of the deposited source code when their supplier defaults to the licensee's detriment; so escrow agreements are usually triggered by the supplier's insolvency or inability to provide maintenance, not by events such as are contemplated here. The NCC are becoming much more flexible on the wording of clauses that trigger the release of software from escrow (and now have one that permits a user to access a copy of the source code in the event of Year 2000 problems) but there is no suggestion currently that companies are drafting escrow agreements that trigger if EMU compliance is not achieved (whatever that may mean, in any particular context) by the failure of a programme to adequately process dealings in euro.

What Areas may be Affected?

Generally

At the end of 1997, the European Commission flagged the following as the   **6.32**
most likely areas to be affected:

(a) Accounting software (general ledger);

(b) Electronic payment systems;

(c) Invoicing and billing systems;

(d) Payroll systems;

(e) Accounts receivable and accounts payable subledgers;

(f) Inventory subledgers, which record the value of the inventory;

(g) Fixed asset subledgers, which keep track of the fixed assets, their value, and calculate the depreciation charge for the period;

(h) Work-in-progress;

(i) Financial planning and budgeting software;

(j) Costing systems;

(k) Enterprise resource planning (ERP) systems;

(l) Treasury management systems;

(m) Legal databases containing financial contracts.

Wholesale Payments and Settlements

The Bank of England has already highlighted that wholesale payments and   **6.33**
settlements is one of the major areas where work is required in order to
establish a U.K. capacity to make payments and settle in euros even though the
U.K. is not an initial participant in EMU. Much work has been done by APACS
and also by the CHAPS banks (who own and run the U.K. wholesale payments
system). Although the U.K. is not adopting the single currency in the first
wave, the U.K. real time gross settlement system (RTGS) will be linked with
other E.U. RTGS systems forming part of the new pan-European system, the
Trans-European Automated Real-Time Gross Settlement Express Transfer
system, ("TARGET").

From the beginning of EMU, the U.K. will have to be able to settle wholesale
payments denominated in euros, both within the U.K. and cross-border.
TARGET should allow this but one of the major problems with TARGET is that
central banks must integrate TARGET with their existing payment systems.

CHAPS, the U.K.'s wholesale payment system, operates in real-time and   **6.34**
with each transaction settled individually across Bank of England accounts to
ensure immediate finality. CHAPS will offer services in euros for its members
and their customers. Membership of CHAPS is open to credit institutions

worldwide which conform to objective criteria. Membership includes share-holder status which ensures a say in how CHAPS is run and developed. In addition to sending payments to other members of CHAPS, payments can also be sent to any bank which is a member of an E.U. RTGS system. Using this route, payments can be sent to some 5,000 member banks.

CHAPS is working on making the U.K.'s Clearing House services fit the euro and APACS are currently enabling their high-value payment network, CHAPS, to deal with the euro. CHAPS handles £500 billion a week, with an average transaction value of £2 million. The CHAPS service will handle euro-denominated payments from the start of the Transitional Period. CHAPS will also be the U.K.'s access point to the TARGET cross-border payment system.

Retail Payments and Settlements

6.35   Clearly, banks in the U.K. will wish to have the ability to open euro bank accounts for retail customers from January 1, 1999 and will want the capability to make standing order and direct debit payments from those accounts.

BACS anticipates a demand for automated retail payments in euro from the beginning of the Transitional Period arising from the employee benefits for multinationals and enabling dividend interest payments on euro-denominated bonds.

The Cheque and Credit Clearing Company is working on a specification for being able to process euro-denominated cheques.

The Credit Card Industry

6.36   APACS' Card Payments Group is looking at the changes the introduction of the euro might make to the U.K. card payments industry — and what may be required to enable card issuers to offer plastic card services in euros if the U.K. opts in. Certain obvious changes would be required such as replacing point of sales equipment in shops which cannot accommodate dual currency oper-ations. The 500,000 point of sale terminals in the U.K. almost all work on an assumption of payments in Sterling and do not have a currency indicator.

Bank Holidays/Timing Differences

6.37   A further point that will need to be addressed is bank holidays/time differences. The differences in bank holidays throughout Europe could cause problems under a single currency. Any clearing systems will have to accommo-date for non-uniform holidays. The obvious time differences between the U.K. and continental Europe will also need to be considered and the appropriate market conventions given effect to in financial systems software.

Accounting Generally

6.38   Some major companies already produce accounts in ECU and have said that they will account in euro at the earliest opportunity. Daimler Benz has been reported as saying that it will convert all its systems to euro on January 1, 1999 when the euro will become its internal currency. Will it be easier for other firms to follow suit or not? If not, when should they make the change? As soon as possible; in 1999; or nearer the time when euro notes and coins become widely used? Commercial realities will determine this for each individual company.

Siemens, two-thirds of whose £35bn worldwide sales are reported to be in Europe, have said that getting locked into the euro early is key. At a single stroke, it will enable them to limit a large amount of their exchange rate exposures and so eliminate a major risk to its business. This approach will also bring with it another major concern about how to pay its thousands of staff spread across a number of countries.

Siemens has already announced its commitment to the euro although, because of its year end, it will not introduce it fully until October 1, 1999. It has already reported its intention to write to its customers and suppliers to say that it will only work in euro after that date.

If a company supplies Siemens or a similarly influential firm which adopts a euro-denominated purchasing policy and they are not within the EMU, the question of what to do about hedging currency exposures is thrown into sharp focus.

Changing Your Accounting Systems

The First Regulation sets out the mechanics of converting from the participating national currencies to the euro, or between participating national currencies. This must be done to six significant figures. In some cases there may be input "masks" (restrictions) in systems which would prevent calculations being made to that number of significant figures. This mask would need to be overcome.   **6.39**

Firms need to ensure that their systems perform the conversion using the published rates, rather than the inverse. Some systems currently use inverse rates to perform such calculations which are then rounded and which would not produce the same mathematical result as using the actual rates as required by the Regulations. The problem is that the rounding methodology used by some existing systems is a function of the computer language on which the system was written; which may not comply with the methodology stipulated by the First Regulation.

Looking specifically at accounting systems, the three main types identified by BASDA are:

(a) **Single currency systems:**

    The accounting software used by the majority of organisations, which do not trade outside their country, will be a simple single currency system which operates with the national currency as the "base currency". The "base currency" is the currency unit in which a financial system processes and stores financial information.   **6.40**

    In normal circumstances, these systems offer all the functionality that most enterprises will ever need. However, when the business is using two different units of denomination, *i.e.* the French Franc and the euro, they have substantial disadvantages because they do not allow the user to input data in a second unit of denomination and cannot generate output in a second denomination, therefore transactions in the euro will have to be translated manually into the base currency before being entered.

(b) **Multi-currency systems:**

6.41   Multi-currency systems offer a number of alternatives. In a system which provides multi-currency input, the user can input data in one of several currency units. The input is stored in both the transaction currency (which in some cases may be the euro) and the national currency or base currency. The software automatically converts the input transactions to the base currency and the books of account are maintained in the base currency.

However, some systems provide only multi-currency output for reporting purposes and require all inputs to be in the base currency. Transaction processing is done in the base currency and output amounts are converted to an alternate currency.

Most multi-currency systems allow input and output in several currencies but, all transaction processing takes place in a single base currency. These systems could use the euro as their base currency and use the national currency units as the transaction currency (or vice versa). When processing amounts denominated in the national currency unit, these would be converted to euro, then processed and finally converted back to the national currency.

(c) **Multiple base currencies:**

6.42   Without doubt the most popular approach for dealing with the advent of the euro is a solution which offers "multiple base currencies". These permit input, transaction processing and output in the denominated national currency unit and the euro unit, complete with an audit trail for each transaction. This enables an organisation to handle both the euro and the national currency from the start of EMU. Final accounts can be produced in either currency, giving the user the option to convert historical data at any time. Ideally, the software will allow dual base currency reporting for the General Ledger, as well as, for example, Accounts Payable and Receivable.

However for most smaller businesses, this is an expensive option and, unless they expect to have a significant number of transactions inside the euro zone after the end of the Transitional Period, the cost could be difficult to justify.

The greatest advantage of the multiple based currency software option is that it will enable companies to take a phased approach to EMU. In this situation, the organisation can report in the national currency unit until a chosen date and then make the euro the primary reporting currency. At the same time it will be possible to continue to produce specific reports in the national currency units and to make comparisons with historical data held in the national currency.

Human Resources

Payroll and pension systems will have to support the transition to the euro in **6.43**
"in" countries. In most cases each business unit will handle this on a national
basis. It is likely that most business units will be able to exercise a measure of
control over the timing of the conversion of their payroll and pension systems
and that these systems will be converted fairly late in the process. After all,
these individuals will not want to be paid in euros until they can spend them
in physical form. However any changes will have to be very carefully tested
because of the sensitivity and complexity of these systems. They also interact
with tax reporting systems. Early planning is therefore necessary.

Conversion of Automated Teller Machines ("ATM's") and other Hardware

There are no immediate issues to address within the U.K. in relation to **6.44**
hardware conversion but there would be issues to address if the U.K. "opt in".

ATM's would need converting to deal with new euro notes — indeed, two
sets of currency during any transitional period for the U.K. APACS have said
the software/hardware changes would take two years. The two main changes
would be to the software in ATM's and modification to the cassettes which
hold the notes.

In addition, all other coin sorting and dispensing equipment (and, indeed,
vending machines generally) would need to change. Other examples include
pay phones, parking meters and gaming machines (such as slot machines), as
well as labelling machines and printers.

Other types of hardware may contain embedded software which would
need to be updated, although its physical design might limit its adaptability.

BASDA Standard Software Specification

Help is at hand, at least in relation to, amongst other things, the problem with **6.45**
triangulation. In March 1998, BASDA published its long awaited specification
for application software changes to give effect to EMU. There has been
considerable uncertainty as to what exactly euro compliance is and the
specification is intended to be a reference standard for both vendors and users
of software.

The key requirements addressed in the specification are:

(a) the triangulation method of currency conversion;

(b) standards for reporting to auditors; and

(c) regulations defining how invoices should be treated.

The specification does not cover all potential aspects of the EMU but is an
important step forward in the context of how to create software which will
work out triangulation. Encouragingly, the specification has been endorsed by

both the European Commission and the Europe-wide accounting standards body, the Fédération des Experts Comptables Européens. From May 1998, software packages will be tested against the specification and successful packages will receive a kite mark.

I.T. Contracts and Euro Warranties

6.46   What, impact will EMU have on I.T. contracts such as software development agreements and out sourcing agreements, etc. It is extremely unlikely that there would ever be any issue with continuity of contract.

If I.T. contracts themselves refer to working days, payment in particular currencies, LIBOR or bank holidays, then minor changes might be required to standard forms as, indeed, will be necessary for standard form loan or bond documentation.

The main point is that if one is seeking a new system, which will have to have the capability to handle the euro, the development contract or software licence under which it is provided should contain some form of assurance of the systems capability to handle the euro.

As time has progressed, one or two industry Year 2000 warranties or definitions of "Year 2000 compliance" have been emerging, but nothing like this has arisen in relation to the euro. This is because it is more difficult to draft such a warranty, as the various things that one would need from software to deal with the euro will vary so greatly depending on what the software is intended to do.

6.47   An example of a general euro warranty might be:

"The contractor warrants that the Software:

(a) is capable of performing all functions required of it by the Functional Specification in more than one currency and for any common currency adopted by one or more countries within Economic and Monetary Union ("EMU");

(b) will comply with all legal requirements applicable to the euro and any market conventions, rules, regulations, industry standards and practices and any matters whatsoever required to give proper effect to EMU;

(c) will process, display and print all symbols and codes adopted by any government or body representing the euro".

A report from the Business Advisory Group sent out by H.M. Treasury in January 1998 concluded that "It is difficult to have an all-encompassing warranty for euro-compliance, since requirements will vary from system to system. Rather, it is a matter of specifying the functions required and ensuring the I.T. will deliver them."

6.48   In the case of the Year 2000, a warranty would ensure that the software will process dates appropriately and will not stop or be adversely affected by the Year 2000 and the leap year in the Year 2000. This is quite narrow. A euro-compliance warranty would have to be much broader. Nevertheless, it is a good idea to be seeking such a clause and it would have to be drafted in very general terms.

As in some cases software suppliers will not sign a general "euro warranty", there is, of course, another way to get to the same end. This will need proper co-operation between the contract draftsman and the author of the various technical specifications for the software.

It is a very common approach, in software development contracts, to seek a warranty that the software will comply in all respects, or in all material respects, with its functional specification. Rather than put in an express EMU warranty, which some suppliers might baulk at, an alternative would be to include a warranty of this nature and make absolutely sure that all the necessary functionality required to deal with EMU-related issues is clearly spelt out in the functional specification. One disadvantage is that if something has been left out of the specification, it will not be something that you can claim for under the contract, whereas under a broad warranty, one arguably could.

Appendix 1

Council Regulation (E.C.) No. 1103/97 of June 17, 1997 on certain provisions relating to the introduction of the euro

THE COUNCIL OF THE EUROPEAN UNION,

Having regard to the Treaty establishing the European Community, and in particular Article 235 thereof,

7.01

Having regard to the proposal of the Commission ([1996] O.J. C369/8),

Having regard to the opinion of the European Parliament ([1996] O.J. C369/49),

Having regard to the opinion of the European Monetary Institute (Opinion delivered on November 29, 1996).

(1) Whereas, at its meeting held in Madrid on December 15 and 16, 1995, the European Council confirmed that the third stage of Economic and Monetary Union will start on January 1, 1999 as laid down in Article 109.j(4) of the Treaty; whereas the Member States which will adopt the euro as the single currency in accordance with the Treaty will be defined for the purposes of this Regulation as the 'participating Member States';

(2) Whereas, at the meeting of the European Council in Madrid, the decision was taken that the term 'ECU' used by the Treaty to refer to the European currency unit is a generic term; whereas the Governments of the 15 Member States have achieved the common agreement that this decision is the agreed and definitive interpretation of the relevant Treaty provisions; whereas the name given to the European currency shall be the 'euro'; whereas the euro as the currency to the participating Member States will be divided into one hundred sub-units with the name 'cent';

whereas the European Council furthermore considered that the name of the single currency must be the same in all the official languages of the European Union, taking into account the existence of different alphabets;

(3) Whereas a Regulation on the introduction of the euro will be adopted by the Council on the basis of the third sentence of Article 109.l(4) of the Treaty as soon as the participating Member States are known in order to define the legal framework of the euro; whereas the Council, when acting at the starting date of the third stage in accordance with the first sentence of Article 109.l(4) of the Treaty, shall adopt the irrevocably fixed conversion rates;

7.02

(4) Whereas it is necessary, in the course of the operation of the common market and for the changeover to the single currency, to provide legal certainty for citizens and firms in all Member States on certain provisions relating to the introduction of the euro well before the entry into the third stage; whereas this legal certainty at an early stage will allow preparations by citizens and firms to proceed under good conditions;

(5) Whereas the third sentence of Article 109.l(4) of the Treaty, which allows the Council, acting with the unanimity of participating Member States, to take other measures necessary for the rapid introduction of the single currency is available as a legal basis only when it has been confirmed, in accordance with Article 109.j(4) of the Treaty, which Member States fulfil the necessary conditions for the adoption of a single currency; whereas it is therefore necessary to have recourse to Article 235 of the Treaty as a legal basis for those provisions where there is an urgent need for legal certainty; whereas therefore this Regulation and the aforesaid Regulation on the introduction of the euro will together provide the legal framework for the euro, the principles of which legal framework were agreed by the European Council in Madrid; whereas the introduction of the euro concerns day-to-day operations of the whole population in participating Member States; whereas measures other than those in this Regulation and in the Regulation which will be adopted under the third sentence of Article 109.l(4) of the Treaty should be examined to ensure a balanced changeover, in particular for consumers;

(6) Whereas the ECU as referred to in Article 109.g of the Treaty and as defined in Council Regulation (E.C.) No. 3320/94 of December 22, 1994 on the consolidation of the existing Community legislation on the definition of the ECU following the entry into force of the Treaty on European Union ([1994] O.J. L350/27) will cease to be defined as a basket of component currencies on January 1, 1999 and the euro will become a currency in its own right; whereas the decision of the Council regarding the adopting of the conversion rates shall not in itself modify the external value of the ECU; whereas this means that one ECU in its composition as a basket of component currencies will become one euro; whereas Regulation (E.C.) No. 3320/94 therefore becomes obsolete and

should be repealed; whereas for references in legal instruments to the ECU, parties shall be presumed to have agreed to refer to the ECU as referred to in Article 109.g of the Treaty and as defined in the aforesaid Regulation; whereas such presumption should be rebuttable taking into account the intentions of the parties;

(7) Whereas it is a generally accepted principle of law that the continuity of contracts and other legal instruments is not affected by the introduction of a new currency; whereas the principle of freedom of contract has to be respected; whereas the principle of continuity should be compatible with anything which parties might have agreed with reference to the introduction of the euro; whereas, in order to reinforce legal certainty and clarity, it is appropriate explicitly to confirm that the principle of continuity of contracts and other legal instruments shall apply between the former national currencies and the euro and between the ECU as referred to in Article 109.g of the Treaty and as defined in Regulation (E.C.) No. 3320/94 and the euro; whereas this implies, in particular, that in the case of fixed interest rate instruments the introduction of the euro does not alter the nominal interest rate payable by the debtor; whereas the provisions on continuity can fulfil their objective to provide legal certainty and transparency toe conomic agents, in particular for consumers, only if they enter into force as soon as possible;

7.03

(8) Whereas the introduction of the euro constitutes a change in the monetary law of each participating Member State; whereas the recognition of the monetary law of a State is a universally accepted principle; whereas the explicit confirmation of the principle of continuity should lead to the recognition of continuity of contracts and other legal instruments in the jurisdictions of third countries;

(9) Whereas the term 'contract' used for the definition of legal instruments is meant to include all types of contracts, irrespective of the way in which they are concluded;

(10) Whereas the Council, when acting in accordance with the first sentence of Article 109.l(4) of the Treaty, shall define the conversion rates of the euro in terms of each of the national currencies of the participating Member States; whereas these conversion rates should be used for any conversion between the euro and the national currency units or between the national currency units; whereas for any conversion between national currency units, a fixed algorithm should define the result; whereas the use of inverse rates for conversion would imply rounding of rates and could result in significant inaccuracies, notably if large amounts are involved;

(11) Whereas the introduction of the euro requires the rounding of monetary amounts; whereas an early indication of rules for rounding is necessary in the course of the operation of the common market and to allow a timely preparation and a smooth transition to Economic and Monetary Union; whereas these rules do not affect any rounding practice, convention or national provisions providing a higher degree of accuracy for intermediate computations;

7.04

(12) Whereas, in order to achieve a high degree of accuracy in conversion operations, the conversion rates should be defined with six significant figures; whereas a rate with six significant figures means a rate which, counted from the left and starting by the first non-zero figure, has six figures.

HAS ADOPTED THIS REGULATION:

Article 1

For the purpose of this Regulation:

7.05

— 'legal instruments' shall mean legislative and statutory provisions, acts of administration, judicial decisions, contracts, unilateral legal acts, payment instruments other than banknotes and coins, and other instruments with legal effect,

— 'participating Member States' shall means those Member States which adopt the single currency in accordance with the Treaty,

— 'conversion rates' shall mean the irrevocably fixed conversion rates which the Council adopts in accordance with the first sentence of Article 109.l(4) of the Treaty,

— 'national currency units' shall mean the units of the currencies of participating Member States, as those units are defined on the day before the start of the third stage of Economic and Monetary Union,

— 'euro unit' shall mean the unit of the single currency as defined in the Regulation on the introduction of the euro which will enter into force at the starting date of the third stage of Economic and Monetary Union.

Article 2

7.06

1. Every reference in a legal instrument to the ECU, as referred to in Article 109.g of the Treaty and as defined in Regulation (E.C.) No. 3320/94, shall be replaced by a reference to the euro at a rate of one euro to one ECU. References in a legal instrument to the ECU without such a definition shall be presumed, such presumption being rebuttable taking into account the intentions of the parties, to be references to the ECU as referred to in Article 109.g of the Treaty and as defined in Regulation (E.C.) No. 3320/94.

2. Regulation (E.C.) No. 3320/94 is hereby repealed.

This article shall apply as from January 1, 1999 in accordance with the decision pursuant to Article 109.j(4) of the Treaty.

Article 3

The introduction of the euro shall not have the effect of altering any term of a legal instrument or of discharging or excusing performance under any legal instrument, nor give a party the right unilaterally to alter or terminate such an instrument. This provision is subject to anything which parties may have agreed.

Article 4

1. The conversion rates shall be adopted as one euro expressed in terms of each of the national currencies of the participating Member States. They shall be adopted with six significant figures.

2. The conversion rates shall not be rounded or truncated when making conversions.

3. The conversion rates shall be used for conversions either way between the euro unit and the national currency units. Inverse rates derived from the conversion rates shall not be used.

4. Monetary amounts to be converted from one national currency unit into another shall first be converted into a monetary amount expressed in the euro unit, which amount may be rounded to not less than three decimals and shall then be converted into the other national currency unit. No alternative method fo calculation may be used unless it produces the same results.

Article 5

Monetary amounts to be paid or accounted for when a rounding takes place   **7.07**
after a conversion into the euro unit pursuant to Article 4 shall be rounded up or down to the nearest cent. Monetary amounts to be paid or accounted for which are converted into a national currency unit shall be rounded up or down to the nearest sub-unit, or in the absence of a sub-unit to the nearest unit, or according to national law or practice to a multiple or faction of the sub-unit or unit of the national currency unit. If the application of the conversion rate gives a result which is exactly half-way, the sum shall be rounded up.

Article 6

This Regulation shall enter into force on the day following that of its publication in the *Official Journal of the European Communities*.

This Regulation shall be binding in its entirety and directly applicable in all Member States.

Done at Luxembourg, June 17, 1997.

For the Council
The President
A. JORRITSMA-LEBBINK

Council Regulation (E.C.) No. 974/98 of May 3, 1998 on the introduction of the euro

---

THE COUNCIL OF THE EUROPEAN UNION,

Having regard to the Treaty establishing the European Community, and in particular Article 109.l(4), third sentence thereof,

Having regard to the proposal from the Commission ([1996] O.J. C369/10),

Having regard to the opinion of the European Monetary Institute ([1997] O.J. C205/18),

Having regard to the opinion of the European Parliament (]1996] O.J. C380/50),

(1) Whereas this Regulation defines monetary law provisions of the Member States which have adopted the euro; whereas provisions on continuity of contracts, the replacement of references to the ecu in legal instruments by references to the euro and rounding have already been laid down in Council Regulation (E.C.) No. 1103/97 on June 17, 1997 on certain provisions relating to the introduction of the euro ([1997] O.J. L162/1); whereas the introduction of the euro concerns day-to-day operations of the whole population in participating Member States; whereas measures other than those in this Regulation and in Regulation (E.C.) No. 1103/97 should be examined to ensure a balanced changeover, in particular for consumers;

(2) Whereas, at the meeting of the European Council in Madrid on December 15 and 16, 1995, the decision was taken that the term 'ecu' used by the Treaty to refer to the European currency unit is a generic term; whereas the Governments of the 15 Member States have reached the common agreement that this decision is the agreed and definitive interpretation of the relevant Treaty provisions; whereas the name given to the European currency shall be the 'euro'; whereas the euro as the currency of the participating Member States shall be divided into one hundred sub-units with the name 'cent'; whereas the definition of the

name 'cent' does not prevent the use of variants of this term in common usage in the Member States; whereas the European Council furthermore considered that the name of the single currency must be the same in all the official languages of the European Union, taking into account the existence of different alphabets;

(3) Whereas the Council when acting in accordance with the third sentence of Article 109.l(4) of the Treaty shall take the measures necessary for the rapid introduction of the euro other than the adoption of the conversion rates;

7.09

(4) Whereas whenever under Article 109.k(2) of the Treaty a Member State becomes a participating Member State, the Council shall according to Article 109.l(5) of the Treaty take the other measures necessary for the rapid introduction of the euro as the single currency of this Member State;

(5) Whereas according to the first sentence of Article 109.l(4) of the Treaty the Council shall at the starting date of the third stage adopt the conversion rates at which the currencies of the participating Member States shall be irrevocably fixed and at which irrevocably fixed rate the euro shall be substituted for these currencies;

(6) Whereas given the absence of exchange rate risk either between the euro unit and the national currency units or between these national currency units, legislative provisions should be interpreted accordingly;

(7) Whereas the term 'contract' used for the definition of legal isntruments is meant to include all types of contracts, irrespective of the way in which they are concluded;

(8) Whereas in order to prepare a smooth changeover to the euro a transitional period is needed between the substitution of the euro for the currencies of the participating Member States and the introduction of euro banknotes and coins; whereas during this period the national currency units will be defined as sub-divisions of the euro; whereas thereby a legal equivalence is established between the euro unit and the national currency units;

7.10

(9) Whereas in accordance with Article 109.g of the Treaty and with Regulation (E.C.) No. 1103/97, the euro will replace the ECU as from January 1, 1999 as the unit of account of the institutions of the European Communities; whereas the euro should also be the unit of account of the European Central Bank (ECB) and of the central banks of the participating Member States; whereas, in line with the Madrid conclusions, monetary policy operations will be carried out in the euro unit by the European System of Central Banks (ESCB); whereas this does not prevent national central banks from keeping accounts in their national currency unit during the transitional period, in particular for their staff and for public administrations;

(10) Whereas each participating Member State may allow the full use of the euro unit in its territory during the transitional period;

(11) Whereas during the transitional period contracts, national laws and other legal instruments can be drawn up validly in the euro unit or in the national currency unit; whereas during this period, nothing in this Regulation should affect the validity of any reference to a national currency unit in any legal instrument;

(12) Whereas, unless agreed otherwise, economic agents have to respect the denomination of a legal instrument in the performance of all acts to be carried out under that instrument;

(13) Whereas the euro unit and the national currency units are units of the same currency; whereas it should be ensured that payments inside a participating Member State by crediting an account can be made either in the euro unit or the respective national currency unit; whereas the provisions on payments by crediting an account should also apply to those cross-border payments, which are denominated in the euro unit or the national currency unit of the account of the creditor; whereas it is necessary to ensure the smooth functioning of payment systems by laying down provisions dealing with the crediting of accounts by payment instruments credited through those systems; whereas the provisions on payments by crediting an account should not imply that financial intermediaries are obliged to make available either other payment facilities or products denominated in any particular unit of the euro; whereas the provisions on payments by crediting an account do not prohibit financial intermediaries from co-ordinating the introduction of payment facilities denominated in the euro unit which rely on a common technical infrastructure during the transitional period;

(14) Whereas in accordance with the conclusions reached by the European **7.11**
Council at its meeting held in Madrid, new tradeable public debt will be issued in the euro unit by the participating Member States as from January 1, 1999; whereas it is desirable to allow issuers of debt to redenominate outstanding debt in the euro unit; whereas the provisions on redenomination should be such that they can also be applied in the jurisdictions of third countries; whereas issuers should be enabled to redenominate outstanding debt if the debt is denominated in a national currency unit of a Member State which has redenominated part or all of the outstanding debt of its general government; whereas these provisions do not address the introduction of additional measures to amend the terms of outstanding debt to alter, among other things, the nominal amount of outstanding debt, these being matters subject to relevant national law; whereas it is desirable to allow Member States to take appropriate measures for changing the unit of account of the operating procedures of organised markets;

(15) Whereas further action at the Community level may also be necessary to clarify the effect of the introduction of the euro on the application of

existing provisions of Community law, in particular concerning netting, set-off and techniques of similar effect;

(16) Whereas any obligation to use the euro unit can only be imposed on the basis of Community legislation; whereas in transactions with the public sector participating Member States may allow the use of the euro unit; whereas in accordance with the reference scenario decided by the European Council at its meeting held in Madrid, the Community legislation laying downt he time frame for the generalisation of the use of the euro unit might leave some freedom to individual Member States;

(17) Whereas in accordance with Article 105a of the Treaty the Council may adopt measures to harmonise the denominations and technical specifications of all coins;

7.12

(18) Whereas banknotes and coins need adequate protection against counterfeiting.

(19) Whereas banknotes and coins denominated in the national currency units lose their status of legal tender at the latest six months after the end of the transitional period; whereas limitations on payments in notes and coins, established by Member States for public reasons, are not incompatible with the status of legal tender of euro banknotes and coins, provided that other lawful means for the settlement of monetary debts are available;

(20) Whereas as from the end of the transitional period references in legal instruments existing at the end of the transitional period will have to be read as references to the euro unit according to the respective conversion rates; whereas a physical redenomination of existing legal instruments is therefore not necessary to achieve this result; whereas the rounding rules defined in Regulation (E.C.) No. 1103/97 shall also apply to the conversions to be made at the end of the transitional period or after the transitional period; whereas for reasons of clarity it may be desirable that the physical redenomination will take place as soon as appropriate;

(21) Whereas paragraph 2 of Protocol 11 on certain provisions relating to the United Kingdom of Great Britain and Northern Ireland stipulates that, *inter alia*, paragraph 5 of that Protocol shall have effect if the United Kingdom notifies the Council that it does not intend to move to the third stage; whereas the United Kingdom gave notice to the Council on October 30, 1997 that it does not intend to move to the third stage; whereas paragraph 5 stipulates that, *inter alia*, Article 109.l(4) of the Treaty shall not apply to the United Kingdom;

(22) Whereas Denmark, referring to paragraph 1 of Protocol 12 on certain provisions relating to Denmark has notified in the context of the Edinburgh decision of December 12, 1992, that it will not participate in the third stage; whereas, therefore, in accordance with paragraph 2 of the said Protocol all Articles and provisions of the Treaty and the statute of the ESCB referring to a derogation shall be applicable to Denmark;

(23) Whereas, in accordance with article 109.l(4) of the Treaty, the single currency will be introduced only in the Member States without a derogation;

(24) Whereas this Regulation, therefore, shall be applicable pursuant to Article 189 of the Treaty, subject to Protocols 11 and 12 and Article 109.k(1),

HAS ADOPTED THIS REGULATION:

PART I

DEFINITION
Article 1

For the purpose of this Regulation: **7.13**

— 'participating Member States' shall mean Belgium, Germany, Spain, France, Ireland, Italy, Luxembourg, Netherlands, Austria, Portugal and Finland,

— 'legal instruments' shall mean legislative and statutory provisions, acts of administration, judicial decisions, contracts, unilateral legal acts, payment instruments other than banknotes and coins, and other instruments with legal effect,

— 'conversion rate' shall mean the irrevocably fixed conversion rate adopted for the currency of each participating Member State by the Council according to the first sentence of Article 109.l(4) of the Treaty,

— 'euro unit' shall mean the currency unit as referred to in the second sentence of Article 2,

— 'national currency units' shall means the units of the currencies of participating Member States, as those units are defined on the day before the state of the third stage of economic and monetary union,

— 'transitional period' shall mean the period beginning on January 1, 1999 and ending on December 31, 2001,

— 'redenominate' shall mean changing the unit in which the amount of outstanding debt is stated from a national currency unit to the euro unit, as defined in Article 2, but which does not have through the act of redenomination the effect of altering any other term of the debt, this being a matter subject to relevant national law.

PART II

SUBSTITUTION OF THE EURO FOR THE CURRENCIES OF THE PARTICIPATING MEMBER STATES
Article 2

As from January 1, 1999 the currency of the participating Member States shall   **7.14**
be the euro. The currency unit shall be one euro. One euro shall be divided into one hundred cent.

Article 3

The euro shall be substituted for the currency of each participating Member State at the conversion rate.

Article 4

The euro shall be the unit of account of the European Central Bank (ECB) and of the central banks of the participating Member States.

PART III

TRANSITIONAL PROVISIONS

Article 5

Articles 6, 7, 8 and 9 shall apply during the transitional period.

Article 6

7.15

1. The euro shall also be divided into the national currency units according to the conversion rates. Any subdivision thereof shall be maintained. Subject to the provisions of this Regulation the monetary law of the participating Member States shall continue to apply.

2. Where a legal instrument reference is made to a national currency unit, this reference shall be as valid as if reference were made to the euro unit according to the conversion rates.

Article 7

The substitution of the euro for the currency of each participating Member State shall not in itself have the effect of altering the denomination of legal instruments in existence on the date of substitution.

Article 8

1. Acts to be performed under legal instruments stipulating the use of or denominated in a national currency unit shall be performed in that national currency unit. Acts to be performed under legal insturments stipulating the use of or denominated in the euro unit shall be performed in that unit.

2. The provisions of paragraph 1 are subject to anything which parties may have agreed.

3. Notwithstanding the provisions of paragraph 1, any amount denominated either in the euro unit or in the national currency unit of a given participating Member State and payable within that Member State by crediting an account of the creditor, can be paid by the debtor either in the euro unit or in that national currency unit. The amount shall be credited to the account of the creditor in the denomination of his account, with any conversion being effected at the conversion rates.

4. Notwithstanding the provisions of paragraph 1, each participating Member State may take measures which may be necessary in order to:

   — redenominate in the euro unit outstanding debt issued by that Member State's general government, as defined in the European system of integrated accounts, denominated in its national currency unit and issued under its own law. If a Member State has taken such a measure, issuers may redenominate in the euro unit debt denominated in that Member State's national currency unit unless redenomination is expressly excluded by the terms of the contract; this provision shall apply to debt issued by the general government of a Member State as well as to bonds and other forms of securitised debt negotiable in the capital markets, and to money market instruments, issued by other debtors,
   — enable the change of the unit of account of their operating procedures from a national currency unit to the euro unit by:

      (a) markets for the regular exchange, clearing and settlement of any instrument listed in section B of the Annex to Council Directive 93/22/EEC of May 10, 1993 on investment services in the securities field ([1993] O.J. L141/27). Directive as amended by Directive 95/26/EC of the European Parliament and of the Council ([1995] O.J. L168/7) and of commodities; and
      (b) systems for the regular exchange, clearing and settlement of payments.

5. Provisions other than those of paragraph 4 imposing the use of the euro unit may only be adopted by the participarting Member States in accordance with any timeframe laid down by Community legislation.

6. National legal provisions of participating Member States which permit or impose netting, set-off or techniques with similar effects shall apply to monetary obligations, irrespective of their currency denomination, if that denomination is in the euro unit or in a national currency unit, with any conversion being effected at the converion rates.

Article 9

Banknotes and coins denominated in a national currency unit shall retain their status as legal tender within their territorial limits as of the day before the entry into force of this Regulation.

7.16

PART IV

EURO BANKNOTES AND COINS

Article 10

7.17   As from January 1, 2002, the ECB and the central banks of the participating Member States shall put into circulation banknotes denominated in euro. Without prejudice to Article 15, these banknotes denominated in euro shall be the only banknotes which have the status of legal tender in all these Member States.

Article 11

As from January 1, 2002, the participating Member States shall issue coins denominated in euro or in cent and complying with the denominations and technical specifications which the Council may lay down in accordance with the second sentence of Article 105.a(2) of the Treaty. Without prejudice to Article 15, these coins shall be the only coins which have the status of legal tender in all these Member States. Except for the issuing authority and for those persons specifically designated by the national legislation of the issuing Member State, no party shall be obliged to accept more than 50 coins in any single payment.

Article 12

Participating Member States shall ensure adequate sanctions against counterfeiting and falsification of euro banknotes and coins.

PART V

FINAL PROVISIONS

Article 13

7.18   Articles 14, 15 and 16 shall apply as from the end of the transitional period.

Article 14

Where in legal instruments existing at the end of the transitional period reference is made to the national currency units, these references shall be read as references to the euro unit according to the respective conversion rates. The rounding rules laid down in Regulation (E.C.) No. 1103/97 shall apply.

Article 15

1. Banknotes and coins denominated in a national currency unit as referred to in Article 6(1) shall remain legal tender within their territorial limits until six months after the end of the transitional period at the latest; this period may be shortened by national law.

2. Each participating Member State may, for a period of up to six months after the end of the transitional period, lay down rules for the use of the banknotes and coins denominated in its national currency unit as referred to in Article 6(1) and take any measures necessary to facilitate their withdrawal.

Article 16

In accordance with the laws or practices of participating Member States, the respective issuers of banknotes and coins shall continue to accept, against euro at the conversion rate, the banknotes and coins previously issued by them.

PART VI

ENTRY INTO FORCE

Article 17

This Regulation shall enter into force on January 1, 1999.

This Regulation shall be binding in its entirety and directly applicable in all Member States, in accordnce with the Treaty, subject to Protocols 11 and 12 and Article 109.k(1).

Done at Brussels, May 3, 1998.

For the Council
The President
G. BROWN

Appendix 2

EMU Protocol published on May 6, 1998 by the International Swaps and Derivatives Association, Inc.

The International Swaps and Derivatives Association, Inc. ("ISDA") has pub-   **8.01**
lished this EMU Protocol (this "Protocol") to enable the parties to an ISDA
Interest Rate and Currency Exchange Agreement or an ISDA Master Agreement
(Multicurrency—Cross Border) (each as "ISDA Master Agreement") to amend
that ISDA Master Agreement to confirm their intentions in respect of certain
matters arising in connection with European Economic and Monetary Union.

Accordingly, a party to an ISDA Master Agreement may adhere to this
Protocol and be bound by its terms by completing and delivering a letter
substantially in the form of Exhibit 1 to this Protocol (an "Adherence Letter")
to ISDA, as agent, as set forth below.

1. Amendments

(a) By adhering to this Protocol in the manner set forth in Section 2 below, a   **8.02**
party (an "Adhering Party") to an ISDA Master Agreement may effect
one or more amendments to each ISDA Master Agreement between it and
any other Adhering Party, in each case on the terms and subject to the
conditions set forth in this Protocol and the relevant Adherence Letter.

(b) The amendments provided for in this Protocol are set forth in Annexes 1
to 5, and each Adhering Party may specify in its Adherence Letter its
preference that one or more of these Annexes are applicable.

(c) In respect of any ISDA Master Agreement between two Adhering
Parties, where at least one Adhering Party has specified a preference
that less than all the Annexes are applicable, that ISDA Master Agreement will be modified only by those amendments contained in the
Annexes that both parties have specified.

2. Adherence and Effectiveness

8.03   (a) Adherence to this Protocol will be evidence by the execution and delivery, in accordance with Section 5(f) below, to ISDA, as agent, of an Adherence Letter by an Adhering Party on or before September 30, 1998.

  (i) Each Adhering Party will deliver two copies of the Adherence Letter, one a manually signed original and the other a conformed copy containing, in place of each signature, the printed or typewritten name of each signatory.

  (ii) Each Adhering Party agrees that, for evidentiary purposes, a conformed copy of an Adherence Letter certified by the General Counsel or an appropriate officer of ISDA will be deemed to be an original.

(b) Any amendment of an ISDA Master Agreement pursuant to this Protocol will be effective on receipt by ISDA, as agent, of an Adherence Letter from each party to that ISDA Master Agreement.

(c) This Protocol is intended for use without negotiation, but without prejudice to any amendment, modification or waiver in respect of an ISDA Master Agreement that the parties may otherwise effect in accordance with the terms of that ISDA Master Agreement.

  (i) In adhering to this Protocol, an Adhering Party may not specify additional provisions, conditions or limitations in its Adherence Letter or otherwise.

  (ii) Any purported adherence that ISDA, as agent, determines in good faith is not in compliance with this Section will be void.

3. Representations

8.04   Each Adhering Party represents to each other Adhering Party with which it has an ISDA Master Agreement, on the date on which the later of them adheres to this Protocol in accordance with Section 2 above and in respect of each ISDA Master Agreement between them, that:

(a) **Status.** It (i) is, if relevant, duly organised and validly existing under the laws of the jurisdiction of its organisation or incorporation and, if relevant under such laws, in good standing or (ii) if it has otherwise represented its status in or pursuant to the ISDA Master Agreement, confirms that representation;

(b) **Powers.** It has the power to execute and deliver the Adherence Letter and to perform its obligations under the Adherence Letter and the ISDA Master Agreement, as amended by the Adherence Letter and this Protocol, and has taken all necessary action to authorise such execution, delivery and performance;

(c) **No Violation or Conflict.** Such execution, delivery and performance do not violate or conflict with any law applicable to it, any provision of its constitutional documents, any order or judgment of any court or other agency of government applicable to it or any of its assets or any contractual restriction binding on or affecting it or any of its assets;

(b) **Consents.** All governmental and other consents that are required to have been obtained by it with respect to the Adherence Letter and the ISDA Master Agreement, as amended by the Adherence Letter and this Protocol, have been obtained and are in full force and effect and all conditions of any such consents have been complied with;

(e) **Obligations Binding.** Its obligations under the Adherence Letter and the ISDA Master Agreement, as amended by the Adherence Letter and this Protocol, constitute its legal, valid and binding obligations, enforceable in accordance with their respective terms (subject to applicable bankruptcy, reorganisation, insolvency, moratorium or similar laws affecting creditors' rights generally and subject, as to enforceability, to equitable principles of general application (regardless of whether enforcement is sought in a proceeding in equity or at law)); and

(f) **Credit Support.** Its adherence to this Protocol or any amendment contemplated by this Protocol will not, in and of itself, adversely affect any obligations owed, whether by it or by any third party, under any Credit Support Document which it is required to deliver under that ISDA Master Agreement.

Each Adhering Party agrees with each other Adhering Party with which it has an ISDA Master Agreement that each of the foregoing representations will be deemed to be a representation for purposes of Section 5(a)(iv) of each ISDA Master Agreement between them.

4. Evidence of Capacity and Authority

Each Adhering Party may deliver to ISDA, as agent, such evidence as it deems **8.05**
appropriate to evidence its capacity to adhere to this Protocol and the authority
of anyone signing on its behalf.

5. Miscellaneous

(a) **Entire Agreement; Restatement**   **8.06**

    (i) This Protocol constitutes the entire agreement and understanding of the Adhering Parties with respect to its subject matter and supersedes all oral communication and prior writings (except as otherwise contemplated or provided in an Annex or elsewhere in this Protocol) with respect thereto.

(ii) Except for any amendment to an ISDA Master Agreement made pursuant to this Protocol, all terms and conditions of that ISDA Master Agreement will continue in full force and effect in accordance with its provisions on the effective date of that amendment. As used in that ISDA Master Agreement, the terms "Agreement", "this Agreement" and words of similar import will, unless the context otherwise requires, mean the ISDA Master Agreement as amended pursuant to this Protocol in accordance with the relevant Adherence Letters.

(b) **Amendments.** Mo amendment, modification or waiver in respect of the matters contemplated by this Protocol will be effective unless made in accordance with the terms of an ISDA Master Agreement and then only with effect between the parties to that ISDA Master Agreement.

(c) **Limited Right to Revoke.** Adherence to this Protocol is irrevocable except that an Adhering Party may, by subsequently delivering to ISDA, as agent, a notice substantially in the form of Exhibit 2 to this Protocol (a "Revocation Notice"), designate a date (an "Earlier Cut-off Date") earlier than September 30, 1998 as the last date on which any counterparty may adhere to this Protocol in respect of any ISDA Master Agreement between them.

   (i) Any designated Earlier Cut-off Date that would otherwise fall on a day that is less than three days following the day on which the Revocation Notice is effectively delivered will be deemed to occur on the day that is three days following the date of effective delivery. Any designated Earlier Cut-off Date that would otherwise fall on a day that is not a day on which the receiving ISDA office is open will be deemed to occur on the earlier of (1) the next day that ISDA office is open and (2) September 30, 1998.

   (ii) Upon the effective designation of an Earlier Cut-off Date by an Adhering Party, this Protocol will not amend or otherwise affect any ISDA Master Agreement between that Adhering Party and a party which adheres to this Protocol after that Earlier Cut-off Date occurs or is deemed to occur. The foregoing is without prejudice to any amendment to any ISDA Master Agreement between two Adhering Parties effected pursuant to this Protocol on or before the day on which that Earlier Cut-off Date occurs or is deemed to occur, which will continue in full force and effect.

   (iii) Each Revocation Notice must be delivered in duplicate, one a manually signed original and the other a conformed copy containing, in place of each signature, the printed or typewritten name of each signatory.

   (v) Each Adhering Party agrees that, for evidentiary purposes, a conformed copy of a Revocation Notice certified by the General Counsel or an appropriate officer of ISDA will be deemed to be an original.

(v) Any purported revocation that ISDA, as agent, determines in good faith is not in compliance with this Section wil be void.

(d) **Headings.** The headings used in this Protocol and any Adherence Letter are for purposes of reference only and are not to affect the construction of or to be taken into consideration in interpreting this Protocol or any Adherence Letter.

8.07

(e) **Governing Law.** This Protocol and each Adherence Letter will, as between two Adhering Parties and in respect of each ISDA Master Agreement between them, be governed by and construed in accordance with the law specified to govern that ISDA Master Agreement.

(f) **Notices.** Any Adherence Letter or Revocation Notice must be in writing and delivered in person or by courier to ISDA at either 600 Fifth Avenue, 27th Floor, Rockefeller Center, New York, NY 10020–2302 or One New Change, London EC4M 9QQ and will be deemed effectively delivered on the date it is delivered unless on the date of that delivery the receiving ISDA office is closed or that communication is delivered after 3.00 p.m., local time in the city where delivery is made, in which case that communication will be deemed effectively delivered on the next day the relevant ISDA office is open.

6. Definitions

As used in the Annexes:

8.08

(a) References to the "1991 Definitions", the "1998 Supplement", the "1992 F.X. Definitions", the "1997 Government Bond Option Definitions" and the "1998 F.X. Definitions" means the 1991 ISDA Definitions, the 1998 Supplement to the 1991 ISDA Definitions, the 1992 ISDA F.X. and Currency Option Definitions, the 1997 ISDA Government Bond Option Definitions and the 1998 F.X. and Currency Option Definitions, respectively (each as published by ISDA or, in the case of the 1998 F.X. Definitions, by ISDA, the Emerging Markets Traders Association and The Foreign Exchange Committee);

(b) "Confirmation", with respect to a Transaction, has the meaning given that term in the related ISDA Master Agreement;

(c) "Transaction" means a Swap Transaction or a Transaction entered into under an ISDA Master Agreement between two Adhering Parties; and

(d) The terms "euro unit", "national currency unit", "participating Member State" and "transitional period" have the meanings given to those terms in the European Council Regulation on the legal framework for the introduction of the euro, which it is currently anticipated will come into force on January 1, 1999.

ANNEX 1

ISDA EMU CONTINUITY PROVISION

8.09   The terms of each ISDA Master Agreement are amended by the addition of the following clause:

"(a) The parties confirm that, except as provided in sub-section (b) below, the occurrence or non-occurrence of an event associated with economic and monetary union in the European Community will not have the effect of altering any term of, or discharging or excusing performance under, the Agreement or any Transaction, give a party the right unilaterally to alter or terminate the Agreement or any Transaction or, in and of itself, give give to an Event of Default, Termination Event or otherwise be the basis for the effective designation of an Early Termination Date.

'An event associated with economic and monetary union in the European Community' includes, without limitation, each (and any combination) of the following:

(i) the introduction of, changeover to or operation of a single or unified European currency (whether known as the euro or otherwise);

(ii) the fixing of conversion rates between a Member State's currency and the new currency or between the currencies of Member States;

(iii) the substitution of that new currency for the ECU as the unit of account of the European Community;

(iv) the introduction of that new currency as lawful currency in a Member State;

(v) the withdrawal from legal tender of any currency that, before the introduction of the new currency, was lawful currency in one of the Member States; or

(vi) the disappearance or replacement of a relevant rate option or other price source for the ECU or the national currency of any Member State, or the failure of the agree sponsor (or a successor sponsor) to publish or display a relevant rate, index, price, page or screen.

(b) Any agreement between the parties that amends or overrides the provisions of this Section in respect of any Transaction will be effective if it is in writing and expressly refers to this Section or to European monetary union or to an event associated with economic and monetary union in the European Community and would otherwise be effective in accordance with Section 9(b)."

ANNEX 2

PRICE SOURCES

In respect of each Transaction entered into before the start of the third stage of **8.10**
European Economic and Monetary Union ("EMU") pursuant to which
amounts are payable by reference to rates for deposits in the ECU or the
national currency unit of a participating Member State (a "Legacy Transaction"), including (but not limited to) Legacy Transactions evidenced by a
Confirmation incorporating the 1991 Definitions (whether or not supplemented
by the 1998 Supplement):

(a) **Disappearance of Price Sources.** The parties recognise that the introduction of the euro at the start of the third stage of EMU may result in
(i) the disappearance of certain published or displayed rates for deposits
in the ECU or a national currency unit used to determine a Relevant
Rate or (ii) changes in the way those rates are quoted and published or
displayed.

(b) **Fallbacks.** Accordingly, the parties agree that, where a Relevant Rate is
to be determined after the start of the third stage of EMU by reference to
a rate for deposits in the ECU or a national currency unit which appears
on a designated display page or in another published source, in
accordance with the Floating Rate Option specified in the relevant
Confirmation, and if the relevant information vendor has ceased to
publish or display rates for deposits in the ECU or the relevant national
currency unit, as the case may be, on or in the designated page or
publication, then the Relevant Rate will be determined in accordance
with the first applicable fallback so that:

   (i) if rates deposits in euros appear on or in the designated page or
   publication, the Relevant Rate will be determined by reference to
   those rates instead; or
   (ii) if rates for deposits in euros do not appear on or in the
   designated page or publication, the Relevant Rate will be determined by reference to rates for deposits in euros which appear on
   or in the successor page or publication, if any, officially designated by the sponsor of the designated page or publication, and,
   for this purpose, the relevant sponsor and any designation it has
   made will be determined where possible by reference to the Price
   Sources Update published by ISDA (the "Price Sources Update");
   or
   (iii) if the relevant sponsor is not identified in the Price Sources
   Update or the sponsor has not officially designated a successor
   page or publication, the Relevant Rate will be deermined by
   reference to rates for deposits in euros which appear on the
   successor page or publication, if any, designated by the relevant
   information vendor; or

8.11   (iv) if the relevant information vendor has not designated a successor page or publication and if the specified Floating Rate Option refers to a published rate for deposits in the ECU or a national currency unit (the "Original Rate") based on quotations provided by banks in the participating Member States (a "Domestic Rate"), the Relevant Rate will be determined by reference to rates for deposits in euros which appear on a display page on any screen service selected by the Calculation Agent and maintained by any recognised information vendor (including, without limitation, the Reuter Monitor Money Rates Service, the Dow Jones Telerate Service and the Bloomberg service) for the display of EURIBOR or, if the Floating Rate Option refers to reference rates for overnight deposits in the national currency unit, EONIA (a "EURIBOR Screen"), for which purpose "EURIBOR" and "EONIA" each means the rate for deposits in euros designated as such and sponsored jointly by the European Banking Federation and ACI—The Financial Market Association (or any company established by the joint sponsors for the purpose of compiling and publishing such rates); or

(v) if the rate for a Reset Date cannot be determined by reference to rates for deposits in euros which appear on a EURIBOR Screen or if the Original Rate was not a Domestic Rate, the rate for that Reset Date will be determined on the basis of the rates at which deposits in euros are offered by four major banks (the "Reference Banks") (1) if the Original Rate was a Domestic Rate, in the Euro-zone, to prime banks in the Euro-zone interbank market and (2) if the Original Rate was not a Domestic Rate, in the interbank market in the place where banks would have been polled for purposes of the Original Rate (the "Off Shore Center") to prime banks in that interbank market, in each case for a period of the Designated Maturity commencing on that Reset Date and in a Representative Amount. The Calculation Agent will request the principal Euro-zone or Off Shore Center office of each of the Reference Banks to provide a quotation of its rate. If at least two quotations are provided, the rate for that Reset Date will be the arithmetic mean of the quotations. If fewer than two quotations are provided as requested, the rate for that Reset Date will be the arithmetic mean of the rates quoted by major banks in the Euro-zone of Off Shore Center, as appropriate, selected by the Calculation Agent, for loans in euros to leading European banks for a period of the Designated Maturity commencing on that Reset Date and in a Representative Amount. For the purpose of this provision, "Euro-zone" means the region comprised of the participating Member States.

8.12   (c) **Adjustment to Day Count Fraction.** The parties recognise that rates for deposits or loans, as appropriate, in euros which appear on or in the designated page or publication, the successor page or publication or a EURIBOR Screen or are quoted by the Reference Banks (the "Replacement Euro Source") may be determined on the basis of a different day count fraction (the "Euro Day Count Fraction") from that on which rates for deposits in the ECU or the relevant national currency unit originally displayed on or in the designated page or publication were based (the "Original Day Count Fraction"). Where the Relevant Rate is determined pursuant to paragraph (b) above and the Euro Day Count Fraction is different from the Original Day Count Fraction, the parties agree that an adjustment should be made to the rate determined pursuant to paragraph (b) above to reflect the Original Day Count Fraction and that Calculation Agent will (i) if the Replacement Euro Source displays alternative rates reflecting different day count fractions, determine the Relevant Rate by reference to the alternative that reflects the Original Day Count Fraction or (ii) if no such alternative is available, make any adjustment to the rate for deposits or loans, as appropriate, in euros obtained from the Replacement Euro Source that may be necessary to reflect the Original Day Count Fraction.

(d) **Preserving Fixing Dates.** The parties recognise that the Floating Rate Option specified in the relevant Confirmation defines the Banking Day or Business Day on or preceding a Reset Date (the "Fixing Date") on which the Relevant Rate for that Reset Date is to be determined. The parties also recognise that the rates for deposits or loans, as appropriate, in euros which appear on or in the Replacement Euro Source may be determined on the basis of a different assumption as to the period (the "Fixing Period") between the Fixing Date and the Reset Date. Notwithstanding this difference, the parties agree that, for the purposes of paragraph (b) above, the original Fixing Period should be maintained and the Relevant Date for a Reset Date will continue to be determined on the Fixing Date.

(e) **Adjustment to Fixing Time.** The parties recognise that the Floating Rate Option specified in the relevant Confirmation defines the time (the "Fixing Time") on a Fixing Date as of which the Relevant Rate for that Reset Date is to be determined. The parties also recognised that the rates for deposits in euros which appear on or in the Replacement Euro Source may be quoted and displayed as of a different time (the "Euro Fixing Time"). Where the Relevant Rate is determined pursuant to paragraph (b) above and the Euro Fixing Time is different from the Fixing Time, the parties agree that the Relevant Rate will be determined as of the Euro Fixing Time.

(f) **Interpretation of Capitalised Terms.** Capitalised terms not otherwise defined in this Annex 2 will have the meanings specified in the 1991 Definitions but will also include terms of similar import that are included or incorporated in a Confirmation for a Legacy Transaction (whether or not that Confirmation incorporates the 1991 Definitions).

8.13

(g) **Calculation Agent.** Whenever the Calculation Agent is responsible for calculating a Floating Rate having regard to paragraphs (a) to (f) above, it will do so in good faith after consultation with the other party (or the parties if the Calculation Agent is a third party), if practicable, for the purpose of obtaining a representative rate for euros as of the appropriate Fixing Time but adjusted if necessary to preserve the Original Day Count Fraction and Fixing Date of the Legacy Transaction, and its calculations will be binding in the absence of manifest error.

(h) **Contrary Agreement.** It is recognised that, following or in contemplation of the introduction of the euro, parties may wish to terminate or settle early one or more Transactions or agree a price source or conventions for one or more Transactions that are different from those that would otherwise apply in accordance with this Annex 2. Accordingly, and for the avoidance of doubt, any agreement between the parties that amends or overrides the provisions of paragraphs (a) to (g) above in respect of any Transaction will be effective if it is in writing and expressly refers to this Annex 2 or to EMU or to an event associated with EMU.

ANNEX 3

PAYMENT NETTING

8.14 In respect of each Transaction entered into pursuant to an ISDA Master Agreement:

(a) the parties recognise that the euro is expected to be introduced as the single currency of the participating Member States on January 1, 1999 and that during the transitional period payments may be made in national currency units;

(b) for the purpose of Section 2(c) (Netting) of the ISDA Master Agreement, the parties agree that, during the transitional period, amounts stipulated to be payable in different national currency units should be treated as being payable in different currencies; and

(c) accordingly, Section 2(c)(i) of the ISDA Master Agreement is amended to insert after the words "in the same currency" the words "but, in the case of an amount of euros (whether denominated in the euro unit or in a national currency) payable on any day during the transitional period, only if stipulated to be payable in the euro unit only or in the same national currency unit".

ANNEX 4

EMU DEFINITIONS

(a) **Euro.** The following definition is included as new Section 1.5(u) of the   **8.15**
1991 Definitions, new Section 3.2(ab) of the 1992 F.X. Definitions and
new Section 3.6(x) of the 1997 Government Bond Option Definitions and
replaces Section 4.3(s) of the 1998 F.X. Definitions in respect of each
Transaction for which it may be relevant:

"(u) **Euro.** "Euro", "euro" and "EUR" each mean the lawful currency
of the Member States of the European Union that adopt the single
currency in accordance with the Treaty establishing the European
Community, as amended by the Treaty on European Union."

(b) **ECU.** The following definition replaces Section 1.5(g) of the 1991
Definitions, Section 3.2(h) of the 1992 F.X. Definitions, Section 3.6(h) of
the 1997 Government Bond Option Definitions and Section 4.3(t) of the
1998 F.X. Definitions, as appropriate, in respect of each Transaction for
which it may be relevant:

"European Currency Unit.

(i) "European Currency Unit", "ECU" and "XEU" each is the   **8.16**
same as the ECU, as referred to in Article 109.g of the
Treaty establishing the European Community, as amended
by the Treaty on European Union (the "Treaty") and as
defined in Council Regulation (E.C.) No. 3320/94, that is
from time to time used as the unit of account of the
European Community. Changes to the ECU may be made
by the European Community, in which event the ECU will
change accordingly.

(ii) Under Article 109.g of the Treaty, the currency composition of the ECU may not be changed. The Treaty contemplates that European Economic and Monetary Union will
occur in three stages, the second of which began on
January 1, 1994 with the entry into force of the Treaty on
European Union. The Treaty provides that the third stage
of European Economic and Monetary Union will start on
January 1, 1999 and on that date (A) the value of the ECU
as against the currencies of the Member States participating in the third stage will be irrevocably fixed and (B) the
ECU will become a currency in its own right. On June 17,
1997, the Council of the European Union adopted Council
Regulation (E.C.) No. 1103/97, which recites that the name
of that currency will be the euro and provides that, in
accordance with the Treaty, references to the ECU will be
replaced by references to the euro at the rate of one euro
for one ECU. From the start of the third stage of European
Economic and Monetary Union, all payments expressed to

be payable in ECU, or sums to be calculated by reference to ECU, in respect of a Swap Transaction, an F.X. Transaction, a Currency Option or a Government Bond Option Transaction, as appropriate, will be payable in, or calculated by reference to, euros at the rate of one euro for one ECU.''

8.17   (c) **ECU Settlement Day.** In respect of each Transaction evidenced by a Confirmation incorporating the 1991 Definitions (whether or not supplemented by the 1998 Supplement), the 1997 Government Bond Option Definitions or the 1998 F.X. Definitions:

(i) the parties recognise that payments in euros may be settled by commercial banks and in foreign exchange markets in a place on a day on which commercial banks in that place would otherwise be closed for business;

(ii) the parties also recognise that, from the start of the third stage of European Economic and Monetary Union, all payments expressed to be payable in ECU in respect of a Transaction will be payable in euros at the rate of one euro for one ECU;

(iii) the parties agree that for the purposes of the definition of ECU Settlement Day, to preserve the existing position, days on which commercial banks and foreign exchange markets are open in a place solely for the purpose of settling payments in euros should not be considered days on which payments in the ECU can be settled by commercial banks and in foreign exchange markets in that place; and

(iv) accordingly, the parties agree that Section 1.6 of the 1991 Definitions, Section 3.3 of the 1997 Government Bond Options Definitions and Section 1.10 of the 1998 F.X. Definitions are amended to insert after the words ''by commercial banks and in foreign exchange markets'' the words ''and on which commercial banks and foreign exchange markets are open for business (including dealings in foreign exchange and foreign currency deposits)''.

8.18   (d) **Business Day.** In respect of each Transaction evidenced by a Confirmation incorporating the 1991 Definitions (whether or not supplemented by the 1998 Supplement), the 1997 Government Bond Option Definitions or the 1998 F.X. Definitions:

(i) the parties recognise that payments in euros may be settled by commercial banks and in foreign exchange markets in a place on a day on which commercial banks in that place would otherwise be closed for business;

(ii) the parties also recognise that, from the start of the third stage of European Economic and Monetary Union, all payments expressed to be payable in a national currency unit will technically be payable in euros and that there may be no readily identifiable principal financial centre for the euro;

(iii) to preserve the existing position where a payment obligation is payable in or calculated by reference to a national currency unit, the parties agree that, for the purposes of the definition of Business Day, days on which commercial banks and foreign exchange markets are open in a place solely for the purposes of settling payments in euros should not be considered days on which payments in a national currency unit can be settled by commercial banks and in foreign exchange markets in that place and that references to the principal financial centre of a national currency unit should continue to bear the same meaning throughout the term of the Transaction; and

(iv) accordingly, the parties:

   (1) agree that Section 1.4(a) of the 1991 Definitions and Section 3.2 of the 1997 Government Bond Option Definitions are amended to insert after the words "settle payments" in the first paragraph and in sub-paragraph (i) and paragraph (a) respectively the words "and are open for general business (including dealings in foreign exchange and foreign currency deposits)"; and

   (2) confirm for the avoidance of doubt that, notwithstanding the introduction of the euro, in relation to each national currency unit:

      (A) references in Section 1.4(a)(i)(A) of the 1991 Definitions, Section 3.2(a)(i) of the 1997 Government Bond Option Definitions and Section 1.18 of the 1998 F.X. Definitions to the "financial centre" of the national currency unit will be to the city there specified until the Termination Date of the related Transaction, whether that occurs during or after the transitional period; and

      (B) references in Section 1.4(a)(i)(D) of the 1991 Definitions and Section 3.2(a)(ii) of the 1997 Government Bond Option Definitions to the "principal financial centre" of a national currency unit will be to the principal financial centre of the national currency unit immediately prior to the start of the transitional period.

(e) **Banking Day.** In respect of each Transaction evidenced by a Confirmation incorporating the 1991 Definitions (whether or not supplemented by the 1998 Supplement) or the 1992 F.X. Definitions:

   (i) the parties recognise that banks may be open for dealings in euros in a place on a day on which commercial banks in that place would otherwise be closed for business;

   (ii) to preserve the existing position where a function is to be performed or a payment obligation is payable in or calculated by reference to a national currency unit, the parties agree that, for

8.19

the purposes of the definition of Banking Day, days on which commercial banks and foreign exchange markets are open in a place solely for the purpose of settling payments in euros should not be considered days on which payments in a national currency unit can be settled by commercial banks and in foreign exchange markets in that place; and

(iii) accordingly, the parties agree that Section 1.3 of the 1991 Definitions and Section 3.1 of the 1992 F.X. Definitions are amended to insert after the words "are open for" in the second line the word "general".

ANNEX 5

BOND OPTIONS

8.20   In respect of each Transaction evidenced by a Confirmation incorporating the 1997 Government Bond Option Definitions:

(a) the parties recognise that an issuer of bonds denominated in a national currency unit may, in certain circumstances, redenominate those bonds into euros;

(b) the parties also recognise that any redenomination of the Bonds in a respect of a Government Bond Option Transaction could affect the theoretical value of that Government Bond Option Transactions; and

(c) accordingly, the parties agree that in order to confirm that the Calculation Agent will adjust the terms of the Transaction as it determines appropriate to preserve the theoretical value of the Government Bond Option Transaction, in Section 5.2 of the 1997 Government Bond Option Definitions:

(i) the heading of the clause is amended to read "Conversion or Redenomination";

(ii) after the words "converts those Bonds into other securities" are inserted the words "or redenominates those Bonds into euros";

(iii) the words "and/or Option Entitlement" are deleted and replaced by the words ", Option Entitlement or such other terms"; and

(v) after the words "prior to such conversion" are inserted the words "or redenomination".

ANNEX 6

FORM OF ADHERENCE LETTER

[Letterhead of Adhering Party]   **8.21**

[Date]

International Swaps and Derivatives Association, Inc.
[600 Fifth Avenue, 27th Floor   [One New Change
Rockefeller Center   London EC4M 9QQ][1]
New York, NY 10020–2302][1]

Dear Sirs,

EMU Protocol—Adherence

The purpose of this letter is to confirm our adherence to the ISDA EMU
Protocol as published by the International Swaps and Derivatives Association,
Inc. on May 6, 1998 (the "Protocol"). This letter constitutes an Adherence
Letter as referred to in the Protocol.

The definitions and provisions contained in the Protocol are incorporated
into this Adherence Letter, which supplements and forms part of each ISDA
Master Agreement between us and each other Adhering Party.

1. Specified Terms[2]

Annex 1	ISDA EMU Continuity Provision	[Applicable]
Annex 2	Price Sources	[Applicable]
Annex 3	Payment Netting	[Applicable]
Annex 4	EMU Definitions	[Applicable]
Annex 5	Bond Options	[Applicable]

2. Appointment as Agent and Release

We hereby appoint ISDA as our agent for the limited purposes of the
Protocol and accordingly we waive, and hereby release ISDA from, any rights,
claims, actions or causes of action whatsoever (whether in contract, tort or
otherwise) arising out of or in any way relating to this Adherence Letter or our
adherence to the Protocol or any actions contemplated as being required by
ISDA.

---

[1] Delete as applicable. The Adherence Letter can be lodged at either ISDA's New York or
European office. See Sections 2(a) and 5(f) of the Protocol.

[2] An Adhering Party may specify its preference that one or more of the Annexes are applicable by
circling or only specifying the word "Applicable" for each Annex that it would like to see
included.

3. Payment

8.22   We enclose payment of U.S. $500, or represent that we have previously made payment of that amount to you, in respect of our adherence to the EMU Protocol.

4. Contact Details

Our contact details for purposes of this Adherence Letter are:

Name:
Address:
Telephone:
Fax:

We consent to the publication of the conformed copy of this letter by ISDA and to the disclosure by ISDA of the contents of this letter.

Yours faithfully,

[ADHERING PARTY][3]

By: _____
        Name:
        Title:

---

[3] Specify legal name of Adhering Party. A separate Adherence Letter should be lodged for each legal entity that is a party to an ISDA Master Agreement and wishes to be bound by the terms of the Protocol.

ANNEX 7

FORM OF REVOCATION NOTICE

[Letterhead of Adhering Party]   **8.23**

[Date]

International Swaps and Derivatives Association, Inc.
[600 Fifth Avenue, 27th Floor   [One New Change
Rockefeller Center   London EC4M 9QQ][4]
New York, NY 10020–2302][4]

Dear Sirs,

EMU Protocol—Earlier Cut-off Date

The purpose of this letter is to notify you that we wish to designate as the last date on which any counterparty may adhere to the Protocol in respect of any Master Agreement between us the following date (the "Earlier Cut-off Date"):

[   ], 1998[5]

This letter constitutes a Revocation Notice as referred to in the Protocol.

We consent to the publication of the conformed copy of this notice by ISDA on and after the Earlier Cut-off Date and to the disclosure by ISDA of the contents of this letter.

Yours faithfully,

[ADHERING PARTY][6]

By: _____
        Name:
        Title:

---

[4] Delete as applicable. The Revocation Notice can be lodged at either ISDA's New York or European office. See Sections 5(c) and 5(f) of the Protocol.
[5] Not to be later than September 30, 1998.
[6] Specify legal name of Adhering Party.

EMU Protocol published on October 8, 1998 by the Financial Market Lawyers Group and the British Bankers' Association

The Financial Markets Lawyers Group ("FMLG") has published this EMU Protocol (this "Protocol") in collaboration with the British Bankers' Association ("BBA") to enable the parties to an International Foreign Exchange Master Agreement ("IFEMA"), International Currency Options Market Master Agreement ("ICOM"), or Foreign Exchange and Options Master Agreement ("FEOMA") (each, including current and prior versions as amended by the parties, a "Master Agreement") to amend that Master Agreement to confirm their intentions in respect of certain matters arising in connection with European Economic and Monetary Union. Accordingly, a party to a Master Agreement may adhere to this Protocol and be bound by its terms by completing and delivering a letter substantially in the form of Exhibit 1 to this Protocol (an "Adherence Letter") to the Chair of the FMLG ("FMLG Chair"), as agent, as set forth below.

8.24

1. Amendments

(a) By adhering to this Protocol in the manner set forth in Section 2 below, a party (an "Adhering Party") to a Master Agreement may affect one or more amendments to each Master Agreement between it and any other Adhering Party, in each case on the terms and subject to the conditions set forth in this Protocol and the relevant Adherence Letter.

8.25

(b) The amendments provided for in this Protocol are set forth in Annexes 1 to 6, and each Adhering Party may specify in its Adherence Letter its preference that one or more of these Annexes are applicable.

(c) In respect of any Master Agreement between two Adhering Parties, where at least one Adhering Party has specified a preference that less than all the Annexes are applicable, that Master Agreement will be modified only by those amendments contained in the Annexes that both parties have specified.

2. Adherence and Effectiveness

8.26

(a) Adherence to this Protocol will be evidenced by the execution and delivery, in accordance with Section 4(f) below, to the FMLG Chair, as agent, of an Adherence Letter by an Adhering Party on or before November 30, 1998.

(i) Each Adhering Party will deliver two copies of the Adherence Letter, one a manually signed original and the other a conformed copy containing, in place of each signature, the printed or typewritten name of each signatory.

(ii) Each Adhering Party agrees that, for evidentiary purposes, a conformed copy of an Adherence Letter certified by the FMLG Chair will be deemed to be an original.

(b) Any amendment of a Master Agreement pursuant to this Protocol will be effective on receipt by the FMLG Chair, as agent, of an Adherence Letter from each party to that Master Agreement.

(c) This Protocol is intended for use without negotiation, but without prejudice to any amendment, modification or waiver in respect of a Master Agreement that the parties may otherwise effect in accordance with the terms of that Master Agreement.

(i) In adhering to this Protocol, an Adhering Party may not specify additional provisions, conditions or limitations in its Adherence Letter or otherwise.

(ii) Any purported adherence that the FMLG Chair, as agent, determines in good faith is not in compliance with this Section will be void.

3. Representations

8.27

Each Adhering Party represents to each other Adhering Party with which it has an a Master Agreement, on the date on which the later of them adheres to this Protocol in accordance with Section 2 above and in respect of each Master Agreement between them, that:

(a) **Status.** It (i) is, if relevant, duly organised and validly existing under the laws of the jurisdiction of its organisation or incorporation and, if relevant under such laws, in good standing or (ii) if it has otherwise represented its status in or pursuant to the Master Agreement, confirms that representation;

(b) **Powers.** It has the power to execute and deliver the Adherence Letter and to perform its obligations under the Adherence Letter and the

Master Agreement, as amended by the Adherence Letter and this Protocol, and has taken all necessary action to authorise such execution, delivery and performance;

(c) **No Violation or Conflict.** Such execution, delivery and performance do not violate or conflict with any law applicable to it, any provision of its constitutional documents, any order or judgment of any court or other agency of government applicable to it or any of its assets or any contractual restriction binding on or affecting it or any of its assets;

(d) **Consents.** All governmental and other consents that are required to have been obtained by it with respect to the Adherence Letter and the Master Agreement, as amended by the Adherence Letter and this Protocol, have been obtained and are in full force and effect and all conditions of any such consents have been complied with;

(e) **Obligations Binding.** Its obligations under the Adherence Letter and the Master Agreement, as amended by the Adherence Letter and this Protocol, constitute its legal, valid and binding obligations, enforceable in accordance with their respective terms (subject to applicable bankruptcy, reorganisation, insolvency, moratorium or similar laws affecting creditors' rights generally and subject, as to enforceability, to equitable principles of general application (regardless of whether enforcement is sought in a proceeding in equity or at law)); and

(f) **Credit Support.** Its adherence to this Protocol or any amendment contemplated by this Protocol will not, in and of itself, adversely affect any obligations owed, whether by it or by any third party, under any Credit Support Document which it is required to deliver under that Master Agreement.

Each Adhering Party agrees with each other Adhering Party with which it has a Master Agreement that each of the foregoing representations will be deemed to be a representation for purposes of each Master Agreement between them.

4. Miscellaneous

(a) **Entire Agreement; Restatement.**   8.28

(i) This Protocol constitutes the entire agreement and understanding of the Adhering Parties with respect to its subject matter and supersedes all oral communications and prior writings (except as otherwise contemplated or provided in an Annex or elsewhere in this Protocol) with respect thereto.

(ii) Except for any amendment to a Master Agreement made pursuant to this Protocol, all terms and conditions of that Master Agreement will continue in full force and effect in accordance with its provisions on the effective date of that amendment. As used in that Master Agreement, the terms "Agreement", "this Agreement" and words of similar import will, unless the context otherwise requires, mean the Master Agreement as amended pursuant to this Protocol in accordance with the relevant Adherence Letters.

(b) **Amendments.** No amendment, modification or waiver in respect of the matters contemplated by this Protocol (including, but not limited to, any Transaction) will be effective unless it is in writing and expressly refers to this Protocol or to the European monetary union or to an event association with economic and monetary union in the European Community and would otherwise be effective in accordance with the terms of the Master Agreement governing amendments and then only with effect between the parties to that Master Agreement.

(c) **Limited Right to Revoke.** Adherence to this Protocol is irrevocable except that an Adhering Party may, by subsequently delivering to the FMLG Chair, as agent, a notice substantially in the form of Exhibit 2 to this Protocol (a "Revocation Notice"), designate a date (an "Earlier Cut-off Date") earlier than September 30, 1998 as the last date on which any counterparty may adhere to this Protocol in respect of any Master Agreement between them.

8.29

    (i) Any designated Earlier Cut-off Date that would otherwise fall on a day that is less than three days following the day on which the Revocation Notice is effectively delivered will be deemed to occur on the day that is three days following the date of effective delivery. Any designated Earlier Cut-off Date that would otherwise fall on a day that is not a day on which the Federal Reserve Bank of New York ("FRBNY") is open will be deemed to occur on the earlier of (1) the next day the FRBNY is open and (2) November 30, 1998.

    (ii) Upon the effective designation of an Earlier Cut-off Date by an Adhering Party, this Protocol will not amend or otherwise affect any Master Agreement between that Adhering Party and a party which adheres to this Protocol after that Earlier Cut-off Date occurs or is deemed to occur. The foregoing is without prejudice to any amendment to any Master Agreement between two Adhering Parties effected pursuant to this Protocol on or before the day on which that Earlier Cut-off Date occurs or is deemed to occur, which will continue in full force and effect.

    (iii) Each Revocation Notice must be delivered in duplicate, one a manually signed original and the other a conformed copy containing, in place of each signature, the printed or typewritten name of each signatory.

    (iv) Each Adhering Party agrees that, for evidentiary purposes, a conformed copy of a Revocation Notice certified by the FMLG Chair will be deemed to be an original.

    (v) Any purported revocation that the FMLG Chair, as agent, determines in good faith is not in compliance with this Section will be void.

(d) **Headings.** The headings used in this Protocol and any Adherence Letter are for purposes of reference only and are not to affect the construction of or to be taken into consideration in interpreting this Protocol or any Adherence Letter.

(e) **Governing Law.** This Protocol and each Adherence Letter will, as between two Adhering Parties and in respect of each Master Agreement between them, be governed by and construed in accordance with the law specified to govern that Master Agreement.

(f) **Notices.** Any Adherence Letter or Revocation Notice must be in writing and delivered in person or by courier to the FMLG Chair and will be deemed effectively delivered on the date it is delivered unless on the date of that delivery the FRBNY is closed or that communication is delivered after 3.00 p.m., New York time, in which case that communication will be deemed effectively delivered on the next day the FRBNY is open.

5. Definitions

As used in the Annexes: **8.30**

(a) (a) References to the "1998 FX Definitions", means the 1998 FX and Currency Option Defintions as published by The International Swaps and Derivatives Association Inc., the Emerging Markets Traders Association and the Foreign Exchange Committee ("FX Committee");

(b) "Confirmation", with respect to a Transaction, has the meaning given that term in the related Master Agreement;

(c) "Transaction" means an FX Transaction or a Currency Option Transaction (which terms shall include the analogous terms in any Master Agreement) entered into under a Master Agreement between two Adhering Parties; and

(d) The terms "euro unit", "national currency unit", "participating Member State" and "transitional period" have the meanings given to those terms in the European Council Regulation on the legal framework for the introduction of the euro, which it is currently anticipated will come into force on January 1, 1999.

(e) "Conversion Rate" shall mean the conversion rate of the relevant national currency unit for the euro, adopted in accordance with Article 109.l(4) of the Treaty establishing the European Community, as amended by the Treaty on European Union.

6. Intent

Nothing herein shall be deemed to affect or have any implications with respect   **8.31**
to the ongoing legal obligations of any Adhering Party or any other party under any transaction to which this Protocol does not apply, the purpose hereof being to provide greater certainty as to the precise application of otherwise generally applicable principles.

ANNEX 1

EMU CONTINUITY PROVISION

8.32   The terms of each Master Agreement (including terms relating to force majeure, acts of State, illegality and impossibility) are amended by the addition of the following clause as a new section of the "Miscellaneous" provisions:

> "EMU   The parties confirm that the occurrence or non-occurrence of an event associated with economic and monetary union in the European Community will not have the effect of altering any term of, or discharging or excusing performance under, the Agreement or any Transaction, give a party the right unilaterally to alter or terminate the Agreement or any Transaction or, in and of itself, give rise to an Event of Default or otherwise be the basis for close-out and liquidation of any Transaction.
>
> An event associated with economic and monetary union in the European Community includes, without limitation, each (and any combination) of the following:
>
> (i)   the introduction of, changeover to or operation of a single or unified European currency (whether known as the euro or otherwise);
>
> (ii)   the fixing of conversion rates between a Member State's currency and the new currency or between the currencies of Member States;
>
> (iii)   the substitution of that new currency for the ECU as the unit of account of the European Community;
>
> (iv)   the introduction of that new currency as lawful currency in a Member State;
>
> (v)   the withdrawal from legal tender of any currency that, before the introduction of the new currency, was lawful currency in one of the Member States; or
>
> (vi)   the disappearance or replacement of a relevant rate option or other price source for the ECU or the national currency of any Member State, or the failure of the agree sponsor (or a successor sponsor) to publish or display a relevant rate, index, price, page or screen."

ANNEX 2

PRICE SOURCES

In respect of each Master Transaction entered into before the start of the third   **8.33**
stage of European Economic and Monetary Union ("EMU") pursuant to which
amounts are payable by reference to rates for deposits in the ECU or the
national currency unit of a participating Member State (a "Legacy Currency"):

(a) **Disappearance of Price Sources.** The parties recognise that the intro-
    duction of the euro at the start of the third stage of EMU may result in
    (i) the disappearance of certain published or displayed rates for deposits
    in the ECU or a national currency unit used to determine LIBOR or a
    Base Currency Rate or (ii) changes in the way those rates are quoted and
    published or displayed.

(b) **Replacement Sources.** All references to LIBOR or a Base Currency Rate
    with respect to a Legacy Currency in any Master Agreement shall be
    replaced with references to euro BBA LIBOR as it appears on or in any
    successor page or publication officially designated by the sponsor of the
    dedicated page or publication.

(c) **Contrary Agreement.** It is recognised that, following or in contempla-
    tion of the introduction of the euro, parties may wish to terminate or
    settle early one or more Transactions or agree a price source or
    conventions for one or more Transactions that are different from those
    that would otherwise apply in accordance with this Annexe 2. Accord-
    ingly, and for the avoidance of doubt, any agreement between the
    parties that amends or overrides the provisions of paragraphs (a) and
    (b) above in respect of any Transaction will be effective if it is in writing
    and expressly refers to this Annex 2 or to EMU or to an event associated
    with EMU.

ANNEX 3

PAYMENT AND NOVATION NETTING

8.34   In respect of each Transaction entered into pursuant to a Master Agreement:

(a) the parties recognise that the euro is expected to be introduced as the single currency of the participating Member States on January 1, 1999 and that during the transitional period payments may be made in national currency units;

(b) for the purpose of each Master Agreement, the parties agree that, during the transitional period, amounts stipulated to be payable in different national currency units should be treated as being payable in different currencies;

(c) accordingly, in the case of an amount of euros (whether denominated in the euro unit or in a national currency unit) payable on any day during the transitional period, such payment shall be subject to the Payment Netting Provisions of a Master Agreement only if stipulated to be payable in the euro unit only or in the same national currency unit; and

(d) furthermore, in respect of any obligation (whether denominated in the euro unit or in a national currency unit) so payable, such obligation shall be subject to the Novation Netting Provisions of a Master Agreement only if stipulated to be payable in the euro unit only or in the same national currency unit.

(e) for the purposes of this Annex 3. "Payment Netting Provisions" means the provisions of a Master Agreement relating to net settlement of Transactions and netting of Premiums and/or other payments and "Novation Netting Provisions" means the provisions of a Master Agreement relating to novation netting of FX Transactions and discharge and termination of offsetting Currency Option Transactions.

ANNEX 4

EMU DEFINITIONS

(a) **Euro.** The following definition is included in Section 1 of the Master Agreement and replaces Section 4.3(s) of the 1998 FX Definitions in respect of each Transaction for which it may be relevant:

> "(u) **Euro.** "Euro", "euro" and "EUR" each means the lawful currency of the Member States of the European Union that adopt the single currency in accordance with the Treaty establishing the European Community, as amended by the Treaty on European Union."

(b) **ECU.** The following definition replaces the definition of ECU (or Ecu) in each Master Agreement and Section 4.3(t) of the 1998 FX Definitions, as appropriate, in respect of each Transaction for which it may be relevant:

"European Currency Unit.

> (i) "European Currency Unit", "ECU" and "XEU" each is the same as the ECU, as referred to in Article 109.g of the Treaty establishing the European Community, as amended by the Treaty on European Union (the "Treaty") and as defined in Council Regulation (E.C.) No. 3320/94, that is from time to time used as the unit of account of the European Community. Changes to the ECU may be made by the European Community, in which event the ECU will change accordingly.

> (ii) Under Article 109.g of the Treaty, the currency composition of the ECU may not be changed. The Treaty contemplates that European Economic and Monetary Union will occur in three stages, the second of which began on January 1, 1994 with the entry into force of the Treaty on European Union. The Treaty provides that the third stage of European Economic and Monetary Union will start on January 1, 1999 and on that date (A) the value of the ECU as against the currencies of the Member States participating in the third stage will be irrevocably fixed and (B) the ECU will become a currency in its own right. On June 17, 1997, the Council of the European Union adopted Council Regulation (E.C.) No. 1103/97, which recites that the name of that currency will be the euro and provides that, in accordance with the Treaty, references to the ECU will be replaced by references to the euro at the rate of one euro for one ECU. From the start of the third stage of European Economic and Monetary Union, all payments expressed to be payable in ECU, or sums to be calculated by reference to ECU, will be payable in, or calculated by reference to, euros at the rate of one euro for one ECU."

8.35

8.36   (c) **ECU Settlement Day.** In respect of each Transaction including any evidenced by a Confirmation incorporating the 1998 FX Definitions:

    (i) the parties recognise that payments in euros may be settled by commercial banks and in foreign exchange markets in a place on a day on which commercial banks in that place would otherwise be closed for business;

    (ii) the parties also recognise that, from the start of the third stage of European Economic and Monetary Union, all payments expressed to be payable in ECU in respect of a Transaction will be payable in euros at the rate of one euro for one ECU;

    (iii) the parties agree that for the purposes of ECU Value Dates, to preserve the existing position, days on which commercial banks and foreign exchange markets are open in a place solely for the purpose of settling payments in euros should not be considered days on which payments in the ECU can be settled by commercial banks and in foreign exchange markets in that place;

    (iv) accordingly, the parties agree that Section 1.10 of the 1998 FX Definitions is amended to insert after the words ''by commercial banks and in foreign exchange markets'' the words ''and on which commercial banks and foreign exchange markets are open for business (including dealings in foreign exchange and foreign currency deposits)''; and

    (v) furthermore, the parties agree with respect to any obligation payable in ECU and falling due on or after January 1, 1999, the term ''Local Banking Day'' in a Master Agreement is modified to mean any day which is an ECU Settlement Day in accordance with the 1998 FX Definitions as amended by this Annex 4.

8.37   (d) **Business Day.** In respect of each Transaction including any evidenced by a Confirmation incorporating the 1998 FX Definitions:

    (i) the parties recognise that payments in euros may be settled by commercial banks and in foreign exchange markets in a place on a day on which commercial banks in that place would otherwise be closed for business;

    (ii) the parties also recognise that, from the start of the third stage of European Economic and Monetary Union, all payments expressed to be payable in a national currency unit will technically be payable in euros and that there may be no readily identifiable principal financial centre for the euro;

    (iii) to preserve the existing position where a payment obligation is payable in or calculated by reference to a national currency unit, the parties agree that, for the purposes of the definition of Business Day, days on which commercial banks and foreign exchange markets are open in a place solely for the purposes of settling payments in euros should not be considered days on which payments in a national currency unit can be settled by commercial banks and in foreign exchange markets in that place and that references to the principal financial centre of a national currency unit should continue to bear the same meaning throughout the term of the Transaction;

(iv) accordingly, the parties confirm for the avoidance of doubt that, notwithstanding the introduction of the euro, in relation to each national currency unit, references in Section 1.18 of the 1998 FX Definitions to the "financial centre" of the national currency unit will be to the city there specified until the Value Date of the related Transaction, whether that occurs during or after the transitional period; and

(v) furthermore, the parties agree that with respect to any obligation payable in euro and falling due on or after January 1, 1999 in circumstances where paragraph (e) of this Annex 4 does not apply, the term "Local Banking Day" in a Master Agreement is modified to mean any day which is a Business Day in accordance with the 1998 FX Definitions as amended by this Annex 4.

(e) **Local Banking Day.** With respect to any obligation payable in euro and entered into before or on or after January 1, 1999 that is originally denominated in euro or is at any time redenominated in euro, clause (i) of the term "Local Banking Day" in a Master Agreement is modified to mean any day on which the Trans-European Automated Real-Time Gross Settlement Express Transfer (TARGET) system is open.   **8.38**

ANNEX 5

AVERAGE RATE OPTIONS

8.39   For any Currency Option Transaction whose terms provide for the calculation of an average rate based upon the rate of any national currency unit in exchange for another currency (the "non-euro currency"), part (iii) of the definition of "Business Day" in Annex 4 shall apply for the purpose of determining whether a day is a Calculation Date (as defined in the 1998 FX Definitions). Unless otherwise agreed by the parties, the average rate under any such Currency Option Transaction shall be calculated by (i) observing the rate of exchange of the euro for the non-euro currency on the relevant date, (ii) converting the observed rate from euro to the applicable national currency unit at the Conversion Rate in order to obtain a rate expressed in terms of the number of units of the non-euro currency per national currency unit, (iii) if the Currency Option Transaction requires the use of a rate of exchange quoted in terms of national currency units per unit of non-euro currency, taking the reciprocal of the preceding rate, (iv) rounding the resulting rate to no less than six significant figures (or such other rounding convention as may be specified under the terms of the Currency Option Transaction), and (v) in all other respects, making such calculations under the terms of the Currency Option Transaction.

ANNEX 6

BARRIER OPTIONS

8.40   For any Currency Option Transaction which is a Barrier Option and for which the In-Strike Price or Out-Strike Price, as applicable, is a rate of exchange of a national currency unit for a non-euro currency (as defined in Annex 5):

1. The Barrier Determination Agent shall make its determination under the Barrier Option based upon the prevailing Spot Exchange Rate of the specified non-euro currency for the euro.

2. In order to make these determinations, the Barrier Determination Agent shall use one of the following methods:

8.41   (a) If the In-Strike Price or Out-Strike Price is expressed in terms of national currency units per one non-euro currency unit, then the Barrier Determination Agent shall either:

(i) re-calculate the In-Strike Price or Out-Strike Price, as applicable, as a rate expressed in terms of the number of non-euro currency units per one euro. In this case, the re-calculated rate shall be equal to: (x) the Applicable Conversion Rate divided by (y) the Original Barrier Rate (where the "Applicable Conversion Rate" is the Conversion Rate for the applicable national currency unit and the "Original

Barrier Rate" is the In-Strike Price or Out-Strike Price of the Currency Option Transaction); or

(ii) re-calculate its observations of the rate of non-euro currency units per one euro in order to obtain a rate expressed in terms of national currency units per one non-euro currency unit (which rate shall then be compared with the original In-Strike Price or Out-Strike, as the case may be). In this case, the rate of national currency units per one non-euro currency unit shall be equal to: (x) the Applicable Conversion Rate, divided by (y) the market rate of exchange observed by the Barrier Determination Agent as the number of non-euro currency units per one euro (the "Euro Market Rate").

In each case, the final rate obtained using method (i) or method (ii) shall be rounded to a number with at least six significant figures.

(b) If the In-Strike Price or Out-Strike Price is expressed in terms of non-euro currency units per one national currency unit, the Barrier Determination Agent shall either:

(i) re-calculate the In-Strike Price or Out-Strike Price, as applicable, as a rate expressed in terms of the number of non-euro currency units per one euro. In this case the re-calculated rate shall be equal to; (x) the Original Barrier Rate multiplied by (y) the Applicable Conversion Rate; or

8.42

(ii) re-calculate its observations of the rate of non-euro currency units per one euro in order to obtain a rate expressed in terms of non-euro currency units per one national currency units (which rate shall then be compared with the original In-Strike Price or Out-Strike Price, as the case may be). In this case, the rate of non-euro currency units per one national currency unit shall be equal to: (x) the Euro Market Rate, divided by (y) the applicable Conversion Rate.

In each case, the final rate obtained using method (i) or method (ii) shall be rounded to a number with at least six significant figures.

Terms used in this Barrier Option Addendum have the meanings given in the Barrier Option Addendum published by the FX Committee in association with the BBA, the Canadian Foreign Exchange Committee and the Tokyo Foreign Exchange Market Practices Committee; provided that for the purpose of this Annex 6 such terms shall be deemed to include any analogous terms under the 1998 FX Defintions or under any confirmation exchanged by the parties.

ANNEX 7

FORM OF ADHERENCE LETTER

8.43   [Letterhead of Adhering Party]

[Date]

Chair
Financial Markets Lawyers Group
59 Maiden Lane — 27th Floor
New York, NY 10038
Attn: Nikki Poulos, Secretary

Dear Sirs,

EMU Protocol—Adherence

The purpose of this letter is to confirm our adherence to the FMLG/BBA EMU Protocol as published by the Financial Markets Lawyers Group ("FMLG") on October 8, 1998 (the "Protocol"). This letter constitutes an Adherence Letter as referred to in the Protocol.

The definitions and provisions contained in the Protocol are incorporated into this Adherence Letter, which supplements and forms part of each Master Agreement between us and each other Adhering Party.

1. Specified Terms[1]

Annex 1	EMU Continuity Provision	[Applicable]
Annex 2	Price Sources	[Applicable]
Annex 3	Payment Netting	[Applicable]
Annex 4	EMU Definitions	[Applicable]
Annex 5	Average Rate Options	[Applicable]
Annex 6	Average Barrier Options	[Applicable]

2. Appointment as Agent and Release

We hereby appoint the FMLG Chair with full power of substitution, and any successor in such position, as our agent for the limited purposes of the Protocol. This appointment is coupled with an interest and is irrevocable. We acknowledge that the agent will also act as agent for other Adhering Parties. Delivery of an Adherence Letter to the agent shall be deemed delivery to each

---

[1] An Adhering Party may specify its preference that one or more of the Annexes are applicable by circling or only specifying the word "Applicable" for each Annex that it would like to see included.

other party for which it is acting as agent. Accordingly we waive, and hereby release such agent, the FMLG and each of its members, the Federal Reserve Bank of New York and any component of the Federal Reserve System and the BBA from, any rights, claims, actions or causes of action whatsoever (whether in contract, tort or otherwise) arising out of or in any way relating to this Adherence Letter or our adherence to the Protocol or any actions contemplated as being required by the FMLG Chair and BBA.

3. Contact Details

Our contact details for purposes of this Adherence Letter are: [. . .]

ANNEX 8

FORM OF REVOCATION NOTICE

[Letterhead of Adhering Party]

8.44   [Date]

Chair
Financial Markets Lawyers Group
59 Maiden Lane — 27th Floor
New York, NY 10038
Attn: Nikki Poulos, Secretary

Dear Sirs,

EMU Protocol—Earlier Cut-off Date

The purpose of this letter is to notify you that we wish to designate as the last date on which any counterparty may adhere to the Protocol in respect of any Master Agreement between us the following date (the "Earlier Cut-off Date"):

[   ], 1998[1]

This letter constitutes a Revocation Notice as referred to in the Protocol.

We consent to the publication of the conformed copy of this notice by the FMLG Chair on and after the Earlier Cut-off Date and to the disclosure by the FMLG Chair and BBA of the contents of this letter.

Yours faithfully,

[ADHERING PARTY][2]

By: _____
        Name:
        Title:

---

[1] Not to be later than November 30, 1998.
[2] Specify legal name of Adhering Party.

Appendix 3

Inland Revenue Press Release 5/98 of January 21, 1998

1. Economic and Monetary Union (EMU): Tax Consequences

The Government proposes to introduce legislation in the next Finance Bill to deal with some technical tax issues arising out of EMU. In his speech to the Bank of England Symposium "London as an International Financial Centre for the euro" the Chancellor of the Exchequer, Gordon Brown M.P., said:

9.01

> "I can announce a further step that the Government is taking to help business prepare. We propose to introduce legislation in the next Finance Bill to help businesses by dealing with technical tax issues arising out of EMU. The introduction of the euro in January 1999 will have implications for some U.K. businesses and there are some tax obstacles which business has identified and which we propose to remove. The Inland Revenue are today issuing a Press Release setting out some proposals for change."

This Press Release:

(a) describes some consequences for the calculation of direct taxes which will arise as a result of the start of the single currency in January 1999, despite the U.K. not joining on that date;

(b) sets out the Government's proposals for some legislation in the next Finance Bill (which might take the form of an enabling power for appropriate secondary legislation); and

(c) invites written comments from interested parties on these proposals, or other tax issues arising out of EMU, to be sent to the co-ordinator for EMU for the Inland Revenue:

> Julian Reed
> Inland Revenue
> Room 507
> 22 Kingsway
> London WC2B 6NR

2. Details

9.02

(a) The Inland Revenue have been holding discussions with the Bank of England and certain representative bodies about the tax consequences of EMU. An agreed statement is attached which sets out how the Government proposes that the tax system will apply in certain circumstances.

(b) When dealing with foreign currency, the corporate tax system broadly follows the accounting treatment. The Government proposes to adopt this approach when dealing with the introduction of the euro. Some technical changes are needed to achieve this result. The Government proposes to bring forward legislation to make the following changes:

— Under existing law a trading company can, subject to certain conditions, elect for its corporation tax liability to be computed on the basis of accounts drawn up in a foreign currency. The Government will bring forward legislation to convert automatically an existing election for a currency which joins EMU into an election for the euro.

— Bonds in currencies which join EMU may be redenominated into the euro. It is the Government's intention that a straightforward redenomination will not normally give rise to a tax change that would not otherwise have arisen. The Government is considering what legislation will be needed to achieve this result.

— There are special rules applying, for the purposes of the legislation on foreign exchange gains and losses and financial instruments, to contracts involving two currencies ("currency contracts"). The Government proposes to introduce legislation to allow these rules to continue to apply to existing contracts if the currencies both join EMU.

3. Some tax issues arising as a result of economic and monetary union

9.03

The following is a summary of some tax issues arising as a result of EMU, whether or not the U.K. participates. The issues addressed are not comprehensive, but are those of immediate concern which have been raised with and agreed by the Inland Revenue.

Discussions on remaining issues continue between the Inland Revenue, the Bank of England and representatives of the following bodies: the International Swaps & Derivatives Association, the London Investment Banking Association, the British Bankers' Association, the International Primary Markets Association, the International Securities Markets Association, the Institutional Fund Managers' Association and the American Banking & Securities Association in London.

3.1 Foreign Exchange Legislation

9.04

Q. The foreign exchange legislation allows a trading company which satisfies certain conditions (an "eligible company") to adopt a currency other than sterling as its functional currency for tax purposes by making a local currency election (under Sections 92–94 of the F.A. 1993 and S.I. 1994 No. 3230). Will eligible companies be allowed to make a local currency election for the euro?

A. Yes. The euro will be allowed as the subject of a local currency election.

Q. Will an existing local currency election in respect of a participating currency effectively carry over into the euro without any action or consequence for taxpayers?   **9.05**

A. The Government proposes to introduce legislation in the next Finance Bill to ensure the continuity of a local currency election for a participating currency.

Q. Will a company which has an existing local currency election for a non-participating currency be able to re-elect for the euro following monetary union?   **9.06**

A. Yes, if it satisfies the conditions in the normal way (that is, if the euro becomes an eligible currency and the existing currency becomes ineligible).

Q. When will the revised local currency elections described at paras. 9.05 and 9.06 above become effective?   **9.07**

A. The election for a participating currency (para. 9.05) will switch auto-matically (as a result of the legislation proposed in para. 9.05) from that currency to the euro for the first accounting period ending after January 1, 1999 when the company in question prepares its accounts in euros. An election for the euro which replaces an election for a non-participating currency (see para. 9.06) will only be effective from the beginning of the next accounting period after it is received. So companies must make an election before the start of the first accounting period to which they want the election to apply.

Q. The foreign exchange legislation contains the anti-avoidance legislation in Sections 135–136 of the Finance Act 1993 which may be applied at the direction of the Board. Respectively, the sections apply where the main benefit of the asset or liability is the accrual of a loss and where the transactions are entered into otherwise than at arm's length. In cases where the conversion of assets or liabilities occurs, or the main economic purpose of the transaction has fallen away, as a result of the introduction of the euro, will the Board seek to apply these provisions?   **9.08**

A. No. Sections 135–136 of the Finance Act 1993 will not be invoked as a result of the introduction of the euro, provided that the Board believes that no abuse is taking place. It should also be noted that the Consultative Document on the Modernisation of Transfer Pricing Legislation proposes that under self assess-ment the requirement for a Board's direction would be removed, so taxpayers would have an obligation to declare when these provisions applied. If these reforms proceed, then taxpayers may rely on this statement in the preparation of their tax returns.

9.09   Q. Unrealised exchange gains on debts which are considered "long-term capital assets or liabilities" may be deferred under Section 139 of the Finance Act 1993. If the assets or liabilities are redenominated in such a way as to appear to give rise to a different asset or liability will such gains or losses be considered realised and therefore ineligible for deferral?

A. The Government proposes to introduce legislation to prevent the relief in Section 139 of the Finance Act 1993 being lost as a result of redenomination.

9.10   Q. A company may choose to hedge a foreign currency asset with a foreign currency liability or currency contract. Under Schedule 15 of the Finance Act 1993 and S.I. 1994 No. 3227 exchange movements on an eligible liability or currency contract may, in the circumstances prescribed, be deferred *e.g.* until the disposal of the matched asset. If such a matched asset is redenominated in such a way as to appear to give rise to a different asset will it cause the crystallisation of any deferred exchange movements on hedging liabilities or currency contracts?

A. It is not the Government's intention that redenomination should cause matching elections to become ineffective. Views are invited on whether legislation is needed to achieve this in practice.

3.2 Financial Instruments Legislation

9.11   Q. The financial instruments legislation provides *inter alia* for the taxation of "currency contracts". It contains a definition (Section 150 of the Finance Act 1994) of "currency contract" which requires payments in different currencies. Will currency contracts involving two currencies that convert to the euro no longer be currency contracts, as only the euro will be involved?

A. No. The Government proposes to introduce legislation to ensure that such contracts will continue to be currency contracts for all purposes of the legislation.

9.12   Q. The financial instruments legislation provides that "qualifying payments" may be paid gross by a "qualifying company" (Section 174 of the Finance Act 1994). Will fixed rate swaps of two currencies which convert to the euro lose this protection, becoming subject to withholding as an annuity or annual payments for tax purposes?

A. No. The Government's intention is that such contracts will continue to be within the financial instruments legislation provided that no abuse is taking place (*e.g.* where a transaction is entered into immediately before conversion to exploit this relief).

9.13   Q. The financial instruments legislation prescribes the payments which may be made under a "currency contract". A contract may allow for other transfers of money or money's worth and still be a "currency contract" provided that the conditions in Section 152 of the Finance Act 1994 are met, which broadly seek to ensure that the relative value of these transfers at the "relevant time" is small. Will conversion constitute a "relevant time" for Section 152 of the Finance Act 1994, causing the issue of whether or not a contract is a "currency contract" to be re-considered?

A. No. Conversion, regardless of how it is achieved, will not be a "relevant time" for these purposes. (Council Regulation (E.C.) No. 1103/97 under Article 235 of the Treaty provides for continuity of contract on the introduction of the euro. However conversion may also be achieved through bilateral legal agreement).

Q. The financial instruments legislation contains anti-avoidance provisions, **9.14** dealing with transfers of value, transactions not at arm's length and qualifying contracts with non-residents (Sections 165-168 of the Finance Act 1994). If conversion to the euro causes there to be a new contract, will there be a re-consideration of Sections 165–168 of the Finance Act 1994 potentially causing adjustment to taxable income to arise under these anti-avoidance provisions?

A. No. Conversion to the euro of itself will not cause anti-avoidance provisions to apply, provided the Board believes that no abuse is taking place. (The removal of the requirement for a Board's direction which is referred to in para. 9.08 above also applies to this legislation.)

Inland Revenue Press Release 110/98 issued on July 29, 1998

1. Preparing British business for the euro: consultation of tax consequences of the introduction of the single currency

The Government will be consulting British businesses and other taxpayers on how transactions involving participating currencies will be treated for tax purposes following the introduction of the single currency on January 1, 1999, Economic Secretary Helen Liddell has announced.

9.15

Announcing the proposals, Mrs Liddell said:

> "The introduction of the single currency on January 1, 1999 will change the way in which business is conducted for many British companies, even though the U.K. will not be a member of EMU.
>
> The Government is determined to assist British business to adjust to these changes as effectively as possible. We are working together with business representatives whenever possible to find out what their requirements are and how we can assist them.
>
> Following earlier consultations, we have already identified some technical changes which need to be made to prevent unitended tax consequences arising from the introduction of the euro in other E.U. countries. Today's proposals will be embodied in draft regulations to be published in the Autumn. The consultation will enable British business to ensure that these changes meet their requirements."

This press Release:

(a) outlines the technical changes affecting direct taxes which the Government proposes to make; and

(b) invites comments from interested parties on these and any other issues that should be covered by the proposed regulations.

2. Details

1. In the light of consultations held to date between the Inland Revenue and certain representative bodies, the Government has agreed that

9.16

technical changes should be made to certain tax provisions. Decisions made after an earlier round of consultations with these bodies were announced in the Inland Revenue Press Release of January 21. The summary below covers both new points and those announced earlier. More details, in a set of "questions and answers" are available in the Annex.

2. The changes proposed will deal with four broad sets of questions;

    (i) the treatment of assets/contracts denominated in participating foreign currencies where redenomination into euros might otherwise give rise to a disposal or transfer or bring forward a tax charge; and the treatment of derivatives over redenominated assets;

    (ii) the treatment of financing transactions involving redenominated assets;

    (iii) the treatment of the costs of redenomination; and

    (iv) the interpretation of the special rules allowing for accounting in foreign currencies for tax purposes.

In general, the Government's approach is to try to ensure as far as possible that the introduction of the single currency in other Member States is tax neutral and therefore does not give rise to a charge or a loss which would not otherwise have arisen.

9.17

3. In relation to continuity of assets and contracts — sub-heading (i), the Government proposes to introduce regulations to:

    (a) ensure that, where assets are subject to a straightforward redenomination, there is continuity for the purposes of tax on capital gains both for the assets and any related derivative contracts within the scope of TCGA 1992;

    (b) provide for the appropriate treatment of any cash payments received as a result of the redenomination of bonds in the hands of investors;

    (c) ensure that redenomination does not disturb the relief on unrealised exchange gains under s.139 of the F.A. 1993;

    (d) provide for continuity of currency contracts and options involving two currencies which convert to the euro;

9.18

4. For financing transactions — sub-heading (ii), such as stock loans and sale and repurchase agreements, involving straightforward redenominations (of bonds), the Government intends to ensure, by regulation if necessary, that the redenominated bonds will count as the "same" or "equivalent" assets for the relevant tax provisions. The Government also intends to introduce a regulation to ensure that intermediaries obtain the appropriate deduction for any charge arising on passing on a cash-payment arising from a re-denomination.

5. On costs on redenomination — sub-heading (iii), the Government proposes to introduce a regulation to allow the costs of redenomination into euros of existing non-sterling capital assets so long as the redenomination involves only the replacement of existing stock and not the issue of increased amounts or of greater value. The Government also proposes to make clear in regulations what costs will be allowable in relation to the redenomination of investments.

6. Finally, in relation to accounting for tax purposes in euro — sub-heading (iv), the Government proposes regulations to ensure the continuity of local currency elections for participating currencies and to allow companies to make a local currency election for the euro before the euro comes into existence, but only for accounting periods commencing on or after January 1, 1999. In addition, it proposes a regulation amending the special rules for computing the chargeable profits of controlled foreign companies (CFCs). The rules lock a CFC into computing profits in the currency used by it in its first relevant accounting period. The proposed regulation will ensure that, where that currency is replaced by the euro, the currency to be used in computing future profits will switch automatically to the euro.

Other issues:

7. Although the consultation with representative bodies has focused mainly on the corporate sector, the Government also intends to use the regulations to deal with any tax issues that may specifically affect other taxpayers, including individuals. It will, for example, take the opportunity to ensure in the regulations that the conversion by U.K. resident individuals of cash holdings of a foreign participating currency into euro will not give rise to a capital gain or loss.   **9.19**

8. The Government encourages those who have comments or questions relating to these proposals, or to other areas which they think may need to be addressed, whether by regulation or otherwise, to write to:

> Bridget Micklem
> Inland Revenue
> Room S23
> West Wing
> Somerset House
> Strand
> London WC2R 1LB

3. Notes for editors

1. Clause 163 of the Finance Bill made provision for the introduction of an enabling power which would allow tax changes that are needed as a result of the introduction of the single currency in other Member States to be made by regulation.   **9.20**

2. The enabling power covers all taxes for which the Inland Revenue is responsible and provides scope to change the law to prevent unintended tax consequences arising when the single currency starts in other Member States.

2. Regulations made under the enabling power will be put into statute by a statutory instrument subject to negative resolution of the House of Commons. This is the normal method used for tax regulations.

3. The consultations which have taken place so far on the content of the regulations have been between the Revenue, the Bank of England and representatives of the following bodies:

  (a) the International Swaps and Derivatives Association,
  (b) the London Investment Banking Association,
  (c) the British Bankers' Association,
  (d) the International Primary Market Association,
  (e) the American Banking & Securities Association in London.

4. *Note:* alongside the work on technical tax questions arising from the introduction of the single currency in other Member States, the Inland Revenue has been working with Customs and the Treasury to consider practical arrangements relating to the payment of taxes in euro. More detail on these questions will be provided separately in a joint Inland Revenue/Customs press release.

4. Annex — further tax issues arising as a result of the introduction of the single currency in other Member States

9.21   The Question and Answer statement below on tax issues arising as a result of the introduction of the single currency in other Member States should be read in conjunction with the Revenue Press Release of January 21, 1998 entitled "Some tax issues arising as a result of Economic and Monetary Union". The statement deals with certain further tax issues arising as a result of EMU that have been raised with and agreed by the Inland Revenue.

   The statement is not intended to address comprehensively all the issues that might arise as a result of the introduction of the single currency in other Member States and does not cover possible tax issues that might arise if the U.K. were to join the single currency.

4.1 Continuity of assets

9.22   Q. In what circumstances will the fact of Monetary Union and/or the redenomination of an asset (*i.e.* a debt security, instruments or contracts) from a participating currency into euro be regarded as giving rise to a disposal, transfer, etc. of the asset (or a derivative over the asset) and an acquisition of a new asset (or derivative) by a taxpayer and in what circumstances will the taxpayer receive continuity of treatment, *i.e.* so that the taxpayer is treated as still holding the same asset or derivative that it has always held?

A. The issue should not be relevant to a company to the extent that it is taxed in relation to the asset or derivative under the foreign exchange, financial instruments or loan relationship legislation. In those circumstances, the Inland Revenue would expect the accounts to be followed (subject to the specific rules in those provisions).

In other circumstances, under the application of the existing law on capital gains, the redenomination could give rise to a taxable gain or loss. However, the Government accepts that it is not desirable for a charge to arise on a straightforward redenomination of an asset consequent on the introduction of the single currency.

It therefore proposes to introduce a regulation to ensure that if an asset is re-denominated in euros and the post redenomination asset is in all material respects the same as the pre-redenomination asset (ignoring the changes reasonably required to give effect to the redenomination), then, where this would not otherwise be the case, the redenomination will not be regarded as involving a disposal or acquisition, and the asset will be regarded as the same for capital gains purposes.

If other changes are simultaneously made to the asset beyond those associated with a straightforward redenomination, then the question of whether those other changes give rise to a transfer or disposal and an acquisition of a different asset or derivative will need to be considered in accordance with existing principles.

Q. How will cash-outs received as a result of a redenomination of bonds be treated in the hands of investors?   **9.23**

A. Any cash received as the result of a redenomination will need to be recognised by the taxpayer. In the case of a person holding the asset as part of its trade or of a company taxed in relation to the asset for example, under the loan relationship or financial instrument provisions, the treatment should follow existing rules.

Where the asset falls under the capital gains regime, under current law cash received may fall to be treated as a part-disposal. However, the Government is willing to accept that small amounts deriving from a straightforward redenomination should not be taxed, and therefore proposes to introduce a regulation to provide a *de minimis* exemption for cash payments received on redenomination as a result of the introduction of the single currency. This should tie in with the proposed regulation on continuity of assets and with current provisions such as the part-disposal provisions on the conversion of securities in Section 133 of the TCGA 92. The Government is still considering the question of the appropriate treatment of cash-outs derived from the repackaging of odd-lots and would welcome comments on this subject.

Note: both Q&A at paragraphs 9.22 and 9.23 do not cover the redenomina-tion of equities and equity-related instruments, since detailed consideration of this issue can only be given once it becomes clearer how the redenomination of equities is to be achieved and since it is not likely that many companies will redenominate their shares in the early days of the single currency. At present, it does not seem that any new capital gains issues are likely to arise in this area, since the U.K. has existing legislation which deals with the capital gains consequences of reorganisations of share capital.

4.2 Equities

9.24   Q. If a U.K. company were to redenominate any of its share capital during the transitional period on the introduction of the single currency into euro and, due to rounding, a payment of cash or an issuance of new stock is required to be made to shareholder, will that payment of cash or issuance of stock give rise to a dividend or distribution?

A. The consequences of redenomination of equities (ordinary shares), preference shares and convertibles, can all be dealt with under the normal rules. A cash payment in respect of shares would therefore constitute a distribution except where and to the extent that it fell to be treated as a repayment of share capital.

A cash payment in respect of securities within Section 209(2)(e)(ii) would also more than likely fall to be treated in whole or in part as a distribution. This treatment will apply equally for conversions of any non-pounds sterling and pounds sterling shares, preference shares or convertibles.

4.3 Options and other derivatives

9.25   Q. In paragraphs 9.11 and 9.13 of the Press Release of January 21, certain guidance is given in relation to "currency contracts" as defined in Section 150 of the F.A. 1994. Will the same guidance apply to "currency options" as defined in that section?

A. Yes.

9.26   Q. An interest rate contract (within Section 149 of the F.A. 1994) must include the right to receive or a duty to make a variable rate payment. A variable rate is one based on a rate the value of which at any time is the same as that of the variable rate of interest specified in the contract, for example PIBOR. Will an interest rate contract, or an option to enter into such a contract which specifies a variable interest rate by reference to a currency which converts to euro such that the original specified rate no longer exists, be regarded as having terminated and been replaced by a new contract or option?

A. Such a change to the subject matter of a contract may cause the contract to be void, voidable, or possibly frustrated. However, the contract may continue to exist for a number of reasons. The changes may be insufficient to cause the contract to be frustrated, by reason of the law under which it is written. Similarly, the change in questions may have been anticipated and be successfully provided for in the original agreement. Alternatively, the contract may remain operative by reason of the bilateral agreement of the counterparties to maintain it, which may or may not technically give rise to a new contract.

It is the Government's intention that a contract which "continues" for whatever reason (including when the new bilateral agreement gives rise to what is technically a new contract) will not give rise to a taxable event provided that the economic substance of the contract is not materially altered. As for assets in para. 9.22 above, the economic substance will be considered to be unaltered where there have been no material changes in the relevant factors.

It should be noted that the contract may be in respect of an underlying instrument which itself is not considered to have continued. In these circumstances the contract will be considered in its own right; the question will be whether, in economic substance, the contract has the same effect as before conversion.

In any event, if the contract falls within the F.A. 1994 regime for derivative financial instruments, and so is accounted for on an acceptable accruals or mark to market basis of accounting, it is likely that the tax consequences of a taxable event will be exactly the same as those arising if there had been no such event.

Q. There may be transactions in futures or options in foreign currencies or in foreign currency denominated equities/debts/other financial instruments which are denominated in foreign currencies which do not fall within Schedule 5AA of the ICTA 1988. However, the effect of the introduction of the single currency and/or the redenomination of assets may be to give rise from that time to a fixed return which is from that point a "guaranteed return". Will the provisions of Schedule 5AA apply in these circumstances? **9.27**

A. Schedule 5AA of the ICTA 1988 applies where the main or one of the main purposes of the transaction in question is the production of a return that is guaranteed. It follows that one looks to the purposes of the parties at the time of entering into the transaction. Accordingly, the mere fact that the return from a future or option becomes fixed as a result of and from the time of the introduction of the single currency would not result in the provisions of Schedule 5AA being applied, unless, in entering into the transaction in question, that was an intended result within the meaning of Schedule 5AA.

Q. Schedule 5AA of the ICTA 1988 deals with the taxation of the profits and gains arising from transactions in futures and options that are designed to produce guaranteed returns. Will conversion constitute a disposal for the purposes of Schedules 5AA, causing any inherent profits and gains to be realised for tax purposes at that time? **9.28**

A. The treatment of a conversion for the purposes of Schedule 5AA will follow that proposed at para. 9.22.

Q. Sections 143–148 of the TCGA 1992 provides, *inter alia*, for the taxation of option contracts which are not taxable under Schedule D (broadly option contracts which do not fall within the Financial Instruments rules set out in F.A. 1994, or within the anti-avoidance rules set out in Schedule 5AA of the ICTA 1988, and which are not held on trading account). Section 144 of the **9.29**

TCGA 1992 will apply for example to an investment company holding an option over shares which qualifies as a financial option. The basic approach (under section 144 of the TCGA 1992) is to treat an option as a separate asset for capital gains purposes except where it is exercised, in which case, its grant (or acquisition) and the acquisition or disposal of the underlying subject matter are treated as one transaction. Will the start of the single currency and/or the redenomination of either the option or the subject-matter of the option be regarded as giving rise to settlement or lapse without exercise of an existing option and the entering into a new one?

A. The regulation referred to in paragraph 9.22 will provide for the continuity treatment for capital gains purposes, where appropriate, both for assets and for derivatives (including options) over assets.

4.4 Financing Transactions

9.30   Q. Where a debt security denominated in a participating currency is redenominated into euros, will the redenominated security be regarded as similar to/ equivalent to/the same description as the original security for repo/stock-lending and related purposes, *i.e.* for the purposes of the following provisions:

(a) Sections 80C and 89AA of the F.A. 1986;

(b) Sections 730A, 730B, 737A and 737C of the ICTA 1988;

(c) Section 263B of the TCGA 1992;

(d) paragraph 15 of Schedule 9 of the F.A. 1996.

A. In the case of straightforward redenominations — see Question at para. 9.22 — the Government will ensure (by regulation if necessary) that redenominated securities will count as similar to/equivalent to/the same description as the original securities for the tax provisions relating to repo and stock lending for all taxpayers covered by Question at para. 9.22. The Government is still considering how the law should apply for financing transactions involving redenominations which would not meet the proposed "same asset" tests.

9.31   Q. Where "cashing out" takes place on redenomination, for example, due to rounding, will payments representative of the cash amounts be treated as manufactured payments?

A. The starting position would be that we would expect the characterisation of the representative payments to mirror that of the payments they represent. To the extent therefore that cash amounts themselves are capital payments, the payments representative of them would not count as manufactured payments.

However, where the person making the representative payment is not taxed on a trading basis, the tax liability may not correspond to the economic effect of his action in receiving cash payment and passing it on. The Government will introduce a regulation so that where cash-outs due as a result of a redenomination are passed on, the intermediary obtains the appropriate deduction from any charge. This will only apply, however, where it is clear that no abuse is taking place in relation to credits for tax withheld (if any) or underlying tax relief.

Note: Both questions at paras. 9.30 and 9.31 do not cover financing transactions involving equities which are redenominated into euro. The treatment of financing transactions involving redenominated equities will be addressed, along with continuity questions, when it becomes clearer how share redenominations are to be achieved. However, insofar as similar issues arise, the Government will wish as far as possible the principles established for transactions involving redenominated bonds to carry over to equities so that in the case of straightforward redenominations, the provisions referred to above will apply.

4.5 Costs of Redenomination

Q. Will costs incurred by a company upon redenomination, as a result of the introduction of the single currency, of securities and equities issued by it be deductible for tax purposes?   **9.32**

A. The costs incurred upon redenominated of a company's loan relationships are already provided for in the existing legislation and will be regarded as charges and expenses within Section 84(3)(a) to (d) of the F.A. 1996.

For other non-sterling securities or equities, which are redenominated as a result of the start of the single currency, the Government believes there is a case for legislating a special relief. Accordingly the Government proposes to introduce a regulation to allow the costs of redenomination into euros of existing non-sterling capital assets (both for traders and investment companies) so long as the redenomination involves only the replacement of existing stock and not the issue of increased amounts or of greater value. This regulation will not apply to costs attributable to any other factor — *e.g.* to other changes made to a security or equity at the same time as redenomination. To the extent that such costs are not attributable to the start of the single currency, their deductibility will be determined in accordance with existing principles.

Q. Will costs incurred by an investor as a consequence of its investments being redenominated as a result of the introduction of the single currency be deductible for tax purposes.   **9.33**

A. As far as the costs of redenomination of investments is concerned, some costs may be allowable under current law as a trading expense or as an expense of management of an investment company, but other would not. The Government therefore proposes to make explicit in regulations exactly what will be allowable.

In the particular case of costs attributable to changes to computer software, the Revenue has already given guidance at paragraph I.M. 664 of the Inspectors' Manual.

4.6 Foreign Exchange

9.34   Q. Will non-trading companies be able to make a local currency election to adopt the euro as their functional currency rather than sterling?

A. No. Non-trading companies will not be able to make a local currency election to adopt the euro as their functional currency.

9.35   Q. It may not be apparent to a trading company that the inauguration of the single currency has made the euro the most appropriate currency for the company's account's until some time after January 1, 1999 or even the start of its first post-January 1999 accounting period. Are there any plans to introduce a "window period" (of, say, 92 days, by analogy with the transitional provisions for the commencement of the FOREX provisions) for the making of an election for euro to take effect from the start of the accounting period of the company in which the single currency begins falls or of the first post-January 1999 accounting period of the company?

A. The Government does not intend to introduce a window period in respect of the timing rules on local currency elections. However, to facilitate the making of elections for the euro, the Government proposes to introduce a regulation which would amend the existing local currency rules to allow companies to elect, prior to January 1, 1999 (*i.e.* before the euro actually exists), for the euro for accounting periods commencing on or after that date. This will put beyond doubt the ability of companies with December 31 year-ends to elect for the euro for accounting periods beginning on January 1, 1999. The Government has already announced that it intends to introduce a regulation to ensure that existing local currency elections in participating currencies are converted automatically to the euro.

9.36   Q. Are there any plans to allow a company with euro-denominated share capital and euro-denominated assets to match these under Schedule 15 of the F.A. 1993 or any extention thereto?

A. No. There are no plans to extend the circumstances in which a matching election may be made.

4.7 Authorised unit trusts — stamp duty and SDRT

9.37   Q. The start of the single currency is likely to give rise to an opportunity for or commercial desire for significant rationalisation of unit trusts. However, the existing provision (contained in Section 95 of the F.A. 1997) for rationalisations of authorised unit trusts to take place without any stamp duty or SDRT charge arising on the relevant transfer of assets expires on June 30, 1999. Are there any plans to postpone that expiration date?

A. An extension of the deadline for these reliefs would require legislation. AUTIF have asked Ministers to consider an extension, for a variety of reasons of which EMU is one, but no decision has yet been taken.

Inland Revenue Press Release 114/98 issued in July 31, 1998

1. Preparing British business for the euro payment of taxes in euro

More details about arrangements for British businesses to pay tax in euros if they wish to do so after January 1, 1999, when the single currency is introduced in 11 other E.U. states, were announced today by Economic Secretary Patricia Hewitt.

9.38

Commenting on the announcement, Mrs Hewitt said:

"The introduction of the single currency on January 1, 1999 will change the way in which business is conducted for many British companies, even though the U.K. will not be a member of EMU.

The Government is committed to helping British businesses to make the most of opportunities which arise. Extending the ability to make tax payments in euro where this is helpful to them is an important step in this process.

Both the Inland Revenue and Customs and Excise already accept payments in foreign currencies. This facility is not widely used at present, but newer, more cost effective arrangements are needed for accepting payments in euro because of the likely greater use of this option after January 1, 1999."

2. Details

The Inland Revenue and Customs and Excise recently carried out a joint survey of 2,000 of the largest taxpayers to find out which intended to pay tax in euro from the start of the single currency. This showed that about 30 intended to use euro to pay VAT and 20 to pay corporation tax or income tax. Both departments are putting in place arrangements to deal with this scale of payments but with the capacity to handle larger volumes if and when the demand grows.

9.39

Both departments are still discussing the details with their bankers but they expect that they will be able to accept payment in euros by cheque, BACS (credit) or CHAPS from the start of 1999. The departments will be charged a fixed amount per day per account for the cost of converting payments into sterling. The cost will be comparatively small in relation to the cost of the departments' banking operations and it will be borne by the Revenue departments.

The taxpayer will be credited with the sterling value which is actually received by the departments after conversion at the prevailing rate. The two departments intend to examine and continue to consult on the precise details of these arrangements, including how best to collect underpayments or repay overpayments which arise as a result of currency fluctuations. Representations on this issue should be sent, preferably by the end of September, to either or both of the following:

Bill Arthur	Ken Pummell
Inland Revenue	Customs and Excise
Spur A, 1st Floor	9th Floor, North Central
Bush House	Alexander House
South West Wing	21 Victoria Avenue
Strand	Southend-on-Sea
London WC2B 4RD	Essex SS99 1AA

These arrangements will apply to all taxes handled by the two departments, from businesses or other tax payers, and will apply to existing liabilities as well as new ones. The arrangements will also apply to National Insurance Contributions. The Inland Revenue are working jointly with the Contributions Agency in agreeing the details.

3. Notes to editors

9.40   More details about the arrangements for paying tax in euro after the single currency is introduced in other Member States were announced by the Economic Secretary, Patricia Hewitt.

In answer to a Parliamentary question, she said:

"The Chancellor of the Exchequer announced in his speech to the CBI on November 10, 1997 that businesses, if they wished, would be able to pay their taxes in euro from January 1, 1999. The Inland Revenue and Customs and Excise are today publishing a joint press release setting out further details of the arrangements and inviting comments from interested parties on any aspects of the proposals."

Both departments already accept payments in foreign currencies although few are made. But newer, more cost-effective, arrangements need to be put in place for accepting payments in euros because of the likely greater volume.

Neither department is currently proposing to make repayments in euro because this would be too costly, and repayments are not currently made in foreign currencies. Nor are there any current proposals for accepting returns of any kind in euro.

Inland Revenue information is available on the Internet:
http://www.open.gov.uk/inrev/irhome.htm

HM Customs and Excise
Press Office
New Kings Beam House
22 Upper Ground
London SE1 9PJ

Further information on the euro is available from the Treasury's euro
website: http://www.euro.gov.uk

Appendix 4

Redenomination, Reconvertioning and Payment Wording for Issues Denominated in National Currencies

---

[EITHER, for currencies known to be participating in the third stage of EMU[1]]   **10.01**

The issuer may, without the consent of the Noteholders or Couponholders, on giving at least 30 days' prior notice to Noteholders [SPECIFY RELEVANT CLEARING SYSTEMS] [THE TRUSTEE] and the Paying Agents, designate a Redenomination Date, being a date for payment of interest under the Notes falling on or after the start of the third stage of economic and monetary union pursuant to the Treaty establishing the European Community (the "Treaty")

[OR, for other currencies]

The issuer may, without the consent of the Noteholders, or Couponholders, on giving at least 30 days prior notice to Noteholders [SPECIFY RELEVANT CLEARING SYSTEMS] [THE TRUSTEE] and the Paying Agents designate a Redenomination Date, falling on or after the date on which [NATIONAL CURRENCY MEMBER STATE] participates in the third stage of European Economic and Monetary Union pursuant to the Treaty establishing the European Community (the "Treaty") or otherwise participates in European Economic and Monetary Union in a manner with an effect similar to such third stage.

[AND, in either case]

---

[1] Austria, Belgium, Finland, France, Germany, Ireland, Italy, Luxembourg, Netherlands, Portugal and Spain.

"Euro" means the currency to be introduced at the start of the third stage of economic and monetary union pursuant to the Treaty.

With effect from the Redenomination Date, notwithstanding the other provisions of the Conditions:

(a) The Notes shall (unless already so provided by mandatory provisions of applicable law) be deemed to be redenominated in euro in the denomination or euro 0.01 with a principal amount for each Note equal to the principal amount of that Note in [NATIONAL CURRENCY], converted into euro at the rate for conversion of [NATIONAL CUR-RENCY] into euro established by the Council of the European Union pursuant to the Treaty (including compliance with rules relating to rounding in accordance with European Community regulations) provided that, if the issuer determines, with the agreement of the [FISCAL AGENT/TRUSTEE], that the then market practice in respect of the redenomination into euro 0.01 of internationally offered securities is different from the provision specified above, such provisions shall be deemed to be amended so as to comply with such market practice and the issuer shall promptly notify the Noteholders, the stock exchange (if any) on which the Notes may be listed and the Paying Agents of such deemed amendments.

(b) If definitive Notes are required to be issued, they shall be issued at the expense of the issuer in the denominations of euro 0.01, euro 1,000, euro 10,000, euro 100,000 and such other denominations as the [TRUSTEE/FISCAL AGENT] shall determine and notify to Noteholders.

10.02

(c) If definitive Notes have been issued, all unmatured Coupons denominated in [NATIONAL CURRENCY] (whether or not attached to the Notes) will become void and no payments will be made in respect of them. New certificates in respect of euro-denominated Notes and Coupons will be issued in exchange for [NATIONAL CURRENCY] Notes and Coupons in such manner as the Fiscal Agent may specify and notify to Noteholders.

(d) All payments in respect of the Notes (other than, unless the Redenomination Date is on or after such date as the [NATIONAL CURRENCY] ceases to be a sub-division of the euro, payments of interest in respect of periods commencing before the Redenomination Date) will be made solely in euro. Such payments will be made in euro by credit or transfer to a euro account (or any other account to which euro may be credited or transferred) specified by the payee or by cheque.

(e) A Note or Coupon may only be presented for payment on a day on which commercial banks and foreign exchange markets are open in the place of presentation and which is a day on which the Trans-European Automated Real-time Gross settlement Express Transfer System is open.

(f) The amount of interest in respect of Notes will be calculated by reference to the aggregate principal amount of Notes presented (or, as the case may be, in respect of which Coupons are presented) for payment by the relevant holder and the amount of such payment shall be rounded down to the nearest euro 0.21.

(g) [ANNUAL COUPONS]: if interest is required to be calculated for a period of less than one year, it will be calculated on the basis of the actual number of days elapsed divided by 365 (or, if any of the days elapsed fall in a leap year, the sum of (A) the number of those days falling in a leap year divided by 366) and (B) the number of those days falling in a non-leap year divided by 365).

10.03

[OR, FOR FIXED RATE SEMI-ANNUAL COUPONS]: The amount of interest payable on each [Interest Payment Date/scheduled date for the payment of interest] shall be half the amount which would be payable if interest were calculated for a period of one year and shall be rounded down to the nearest euro 0.01. If interest is required to be calculated for a period of less than half a year, it will be calculated on the basis of the actual number of days elapsed divided by 365 (or, if any of the days elapsed fall in a leap year, the sum of (A) the number of those days falling in a leap year divided by 366) and (B) the number of those days falling in a non-leap year divided by 365).

Provisions relating to the Notes while in Global Form

Following redenomination of the Notes pursuant to Condition, the amount of interest due in respect of Notes represented by the Global Note will be calculated by reference to the aggregate principal amount of such Notes and the amount of such payment shall be rounded down to the nearest euro 0.01.

10.04

Appendix 5

International Paying Agents Association Recommendation of June 12, 1998

IPAA, The International Paying Agents Association, announces today its recommendations to issuers of international capital market debt in preparation for the introduction of the euro.

Many Eurobond issuers are including in their new issue documentation terms for redenomination into the euro. Issuers are also looking at whether or not to redenominate existing debt in legacy currencies. The IPAA believes that wherever possible a consistent approach should be adopted towards the procedures employed. This is particularly important since many of the Association's member's work with the same issuers and clearing systems, and coherent procedures should help to avoid confusion.

None of the recommendations are intended to conflict with the principle of "no compulsion, no prohibition" or to limit the rights of issuers or noteholders in any way. They are simply practical suggestions for the new environment where it is anticipated that the wholesale market will predominantly use the euro rather than existing national currency units after January 1, 1999.

11.01

Recommendations to issuers

The IPPA recommends that:

1. For all international debt instruments, payments of interest and principal amounts due in the national currency units of those countries participating in European Monetary Union as from January 1, 1999 are made by issuers to the Fiscal/Principal Paying Agent in euro.

2. Corporate debt is not redenominated.

3. If corporate debt is redenominated, it is not reconventioned.

4. If corporate debt is redenominated, reconventioned or renominalised, the process should take place on an interest payment date after January 1, 1999.

11.02

5. Interest on redenominated and non-redenominated issues in definitive note form will be calculated on the specified denomination of the notes.

6. Interest on redenominated and non-redenominated issues in permanent global note form will be calculated on the total principle amount outstanding.

7. Payment of interest and principal on non-redenominated issues in definitive note form will be made by Paying Agents to noteholders in the amount specified per note, in accordance with the Terms and Conditions, in either the legacy currency or in euro, according to noteholder preference. If a noteholder requests payment in a legacy currency, the agent to whom the noteholder makes the claim will make the conversion from euro into a legacy currency at no conversion cost to the holder. It is expected that definitive notes held by the clearing systems will be paid in euro.[1]

11.03

8. Payment of interest and principal on non-denominated issues in permanent global note form held in the clearing systems will be paid to the clearing systems in euro.[1]

9. For issues redenominated into euro which are to be reprinted in definitive note form, the minimum denomination should be not less than that on which interest of at least euro 0.01 can be calculated.

10. For new euro issues the minimum denomination should be euro 1,000, in accordance with market practice for other currencies.

11. If redenominating outstanding debt, the issuer will inform the relevant parties of no less than the following specifications:

- original ISIN
- new ISIN, if any (clearing systems/paying agent to provide at request of issuer)
- redenomination date
- redenomination method (*e.g.* book entry/physical exchange)
- redenomination basis (*e.g.* per minimum denomination)
- new minimum denomination
- rounding rules (*e.g.* nearest cent)
- cash compensation (if applied to fractional portions of redenominated securities)
- cash compensation tax treatment
- calculations and payments cannot be made by investor holding by the Paying Agents since this is not information to which they have access.

---

[1] Payments in euro on non-redenominated debt will be calculated by applying the fixed conversion rate.

Index

(All references are to paragraph number)